"This delightful study of Jesus Christ the *man* probes deep and complex truths with a lucid clarity designed for ordinary Christian readers. I'm tempted to say that this is Warfield's christology rewritten for the devout layperson who wants to understand Jesus better and thereby trust, obey, and love him more wholeheartedly. The discussion questions at the end of each chapter promise that the book will be used widely in churches where one of the passions is to understand historic Christian truth in a fashion that is biblically faithful and spiritually nourishing."

D. A. Carson, Research Professor of New Testament, Trinity Evangelical Divinity School

"This is a simple, readable, accessible, and biblical introduction to the divinity and humanity of Jesus Christ. It takes a great theologian with a pastor's heart to boil down difficult big ideas like this."

Mark Driscoll, Founding and Preaching Pastor, Mars Hill Church, Seattle, Washington; Founder, Resurgence; Co-founder, Acts 29; *New York Times* best-selling author

"'Marvel and wonder and worship.' Bruce Ware rightly suggests that this is the appropriate response as we consider the implications of the humanity of Christ. My heart has been deeply stirred through reading this book and contemplating this oft-overlooked but vital aspect of our Savior."

Nancy Leigh DeMoss, author, *Revive Our Hearts*; radio host

"Evangelicals who believe the Scriptures to be God's inerrant Word run the risk of emphasizing the deity of the Lord Jesus and, quite unintentionally no doubt, deemphasizing his humanity. Bruce Ware provides a healthy antidote to this malady. This is a welcome addition to the study of christology and one that will aid in our understanding of and love for the man Christ Jesus."

Daniel L. Akin, president, Southeastern Baptist Theological Seminary

"In far too many instances, the church is functionally docetic, basically affirming that the divine Christ only *seemed* to be human. But as Bruce Ware skillfully and passionately explains, the gospel and its implications depend upon the full deity and true humanity of Jesus Christ. Biblically faithful, theologically solid, devotionally heartwarming, *The Man Christ Jesus* will increase your knowledge of and reverence for our wonderful Savior and Lord, the God-man Jesus Christ."

Todd Miles, Associate Professor of Theology, Western Seminary

"Many arguments have been developed and many books have been written in defense of the full deity of the Son of God. As for arguments and writings in support of the full humanity of the Son incarnate, less attention has been given. Bruce Ware corrects this imbalance by offering a treatment that is biblical, readable, in tune with contemporary issues, and immensely practical. As readers make their way through this book, they will not only become convinced of the humanity of the God-man and understand why the incarnation was needed; they will also be prompted to offer praise and thanksgiving to God for his wonderful work of salvation through Jesus Christ!"

Gregg Allison, Professor of Christian Theology, The Southern Baptist Theological Seminary

"A thoughtful, provocative work that considers the grand miracle of the one who is fully God pouring himself out to become fully man. This book will move you to contemplate and marvel at the wonder of it all."

Mary A. Kassian, Professor of Women's Studies, The Southern Baptist Theological Seminary; Author, *Girls Gone Wise*

"The proper understanding of Christ's humanity is absolutely essential to understanding our calling and ministry. For years I have taught the humanity of Christ, and countless numbers have said that nothing causes them to love Jesus more than a biblical understanding of his humanity. Because of this, I highly commend this book to you!"

Dann Spader, President, Global Youth Initiative; Founder, Sonlife Ministries; author, *Walking as Jesus Walked* and *The Everyday Commission*

"Ever since the church confronted Gnosticism, the reality and necessity of Christ's humanity has been at the heart of Christian orthodoxy. Bruce Ware's grasp and exposition of this essential doctrine contains a rigorous theological precision, communicates an attractive piety, presses the reader to investigate just how central this is to the entire spectrum of the redemptive work of the Messiah, and opens the doctrine to some thick and provocative applicatory ideas. Both ancient and right up to date, Ware's treatment deserves a serious reading."

Thomas J. Nettles, Professor of Historical Theology, The Southern Baptist Theological Seminary; author, *By His Grace and for His Glory*

THE MAN CHRIST JESUS

THE MAN
CHRIST JESUS

Theological Reflections on the Humanity of Christ

BRUCE A. WARE

WHEATON, ILLINOIS

Trade paperback ISBN: 978-1-4335-1305-3
PDF ISBN: 978-1-4335-1306-0
Mobipocket ISBN: 978-1-4335-1307-7
ePub ISBN: 978-1-4335-2416-5

Library of Congress Cataloging-in-Publication Data

Ware, Bruce A.
The man Christ Jesus : theological questions on the humanity of
Christ / Bruce A. Ware.
    p. cm.
Includes bibliographical references and index.
ISBN 978-1-4335-1305-3
1. Jesus Christ—Humanity. I. Title.
BT218.W37   2013
232'.8—dc23   2012015396

Crossway is a publishing ministry of Good News Publishers.

To
Wayne and Bonnie Pickens
with deep gratitude for their lives and ministries,
which reflect much of the character and service of Christ

CONTENTS

Preface: Why the Humanity of the God-Man Matters   11

1   Taking on Human Nature   15

2   Empowered by the Spirit   31

3   Increasing in Wisdom   47

4   Growing in Faith   59

5   Resisting Temptation   73

6   Living as a Man   91

7   Dying in Our Place   111

8   Raised, Reigning, and Returning in Victory   129

General Index   149

Scripture Index   153

PREFACE:
WHY THE HUMANITY OF
THE GOD-MAN MATTERS

*For there is one God, and there is one mediator between God and men,
the man Christ Jesus.*

1 TIMOTHY 2:5

I recall a disturbing moment in my young Christian life. I was about
ten years old, reading my Bible at home, sitting on the middle of my
bed. My pastor and parents had encouraged the youth to be more diligent in Bible reading. Over a period of months I had made it through
parts of the Gospels and some of the Epistles, and I now found myself
reading 1 Peter. Despite the serious and repeated warnings about suffering for Christ, I was making it through this book pretty well. But
then I read 1 Peter 2:21–23, which, in my small, black, red-letter King
James Version (I still have it!) says:

> For even hereunto were ye called: because Christ also suffered for us,
> leaving us an example, that ye should follow his steps: Who did no
> sin, neither was guile found in his mouth: Who, when he was reviled,
> reviled not again; when he suffered, he threatened not; but committed
> himself to him that judgeth righteously.

It is hard to describe how unfair I felt this passage to be. I really
was quite disturbed, not about the part that speaks of Christ's suffering for us and committing his life to the Father, but about his followers' being called to follow in his steps. No fair, I determined. Especially
when the passage says to follow in the steps of one *"who did no sin."*

This was totally outlandish and unreasonable, and I just couldn't see how God could really mean for us to take it seriously.

Behind my childish outrage at what this passage commanded was this: I had been taught in Sunday school that Jesus was God. I remember being quite amazed when I first learned this, that even though Jesus walked this earth and ate and drank and got tired and slept, he was nonetheless fully God. I was taught that the Father sent his Son into the world, and when the Son came, born of Mary, he was still the Son and so he was still fully God.

In my ten-year-old mind, I just couldn't see how it would be fair, then, for God to call us to follow in the steps of Jesus, especially not to sin or to be angry at others who hurt us, since *Jesus was God and we are not!*

Little did I know how this question would come back to challenge me many years later, when I began to study my Bible more seriously and think more deeply about theological matters. This question returned to my mind during my seminary years, when I learned in greater depth that Jesus was both God and man. And that simple understanding— that he had two natures, one divine and one human—began a process of thinking again about 1 Peter 2:21–23 with new questions in my mind: Could it be that even though Jesus was fully God, he lived his life fundamentally as a man? Could the command to follow in his steps be legitimate because he lived a human life in obedience to his Father as we also are called to do? What, then, happens to his divine nature when he takes on human nature? Could he really have been both fully God and fully man and yet lived as one person?

The book you hold in your hands expresses some of the ways that God, in his abundant mercy, has allowed me to process these questions through deeper and richer study of his Word. I want to present here some of the evidence from Old and New Testaments that the human life of Jesus is real and to show how important it is that he lived our life in order to die our death and be forever "the man Christ Jesus" (1 Tim. 2:5) who intercedes for us and reigns over us.

I long for Jesus to be honored through the reflections upon his humanity in this book. Please understand that this is *not* a complete

Christology. I do not in any manner intend to "slight" the importance of the deity of Christ for an understanding of who Jesus was and is, even though his deity is not our focus here. There are a few times when we will examine some aspects of the deity of Christ simply because these must be seen to understand aspects of his humanity. My sense, though, is that evangelicals understand better Christ's deity than they do his humanity, and so my focus here will be on the latter.[1]

I wish also briefly to express thanks to some who have assisted and encouraged me in my writing. Allan Fisher of Crossway first suggested the idea of this book, and he has patiently awaited its completion. I am deeply grateful for the excellent team at Crossway and consider it an honor to publish with them. My family members— Jodi, Rachel, Bethany, and Owen—have all been very supportive and helpful. As any writer can testify, time writing means time not spent with others. Writing is a lonely exercise, and my family has shown such understanding and patience with me, for which I am grateful. Southern Seminary also provided a sabbatical in which I was able to get much done on this book as well as several other projects.

And finally I wish to express my love and appreciation to the two people to whom this book is dedicated: Wayne and Bonnie Pickens. Bonnie is my sister, my only sibling, and I have long loved and admired this godly woman. She is one of the finest pastors' wives I've seen in operation, and I am deeply grateful for her commitment to Christ, to her family, and to the ministry God has given her serving alongside of Wayne. Wayne currently pastors First Baptist Church, La Grande, Oregon. I grew to love Wayne early in his being my brother-in-law, because he loved the Bible, loved theology, and loved to talk and laugh, and he has loved my sister so well. He's an excellent pastor, preacher, and lover of souls, and I count him among my dearest and closest friends.

Jesus Christ is truly amazing. I know only too well my own inadequacies in conveying the depth and breadth and height and length of his greatness, but my hope is that the pages of this book will point,

---

[1] For an excellent treatment of the deity of Christ, see Murray J. Harris, *Jesus as God: The New Testament Use of* Theos *in Reference to Jesus* (Grand Rapids, MI: Baker, 1992).

at least, to some of the ways and reasons he should be praised and thanked and honored and obeyed. My prayer is that the Spirit, who came to glorify Jesus (John 16:14), will be pleased to help all of us know him better, that we may do now what all will do one day in the future: bow our knees and confess with our mouths that Jesus Christ is Lord, "to the glory of God the Father" (Phil. 2:11).

1

TAKING ON HUMAN NATURE

Have this mind among yourselves, which is yours in Christ Jesus, who, though he was in the form of God, did not count equality with God a thing to be grasped, but emptied himself, by taking the form of a servant, being born in the likeness of men. And being found in human form, he humbled himself by becoming obedient to the point of death, even death on a cross.

PHILIPPIANS 2:5-8

Whereas the eternal Son of the Father, the second person of the Trinity, had no beginning and will have no end, the incarnate Son—the son of David, the son of Mary, the Messiah—had a beginning in time and space. This Son,[1] Jesus the Christ, was brought into being through the power of the Holy Spirit, as the divine nature of the eternal Son was miraculously joined together with a created human nature in the womb of the Virgin Mary. Luke's account of this miracle—the grand miracle, as C. S. Lewis rightly called it—is riveting. Luke writes:

> In the sixth month the angel Gabriel was sent from God to a city of Galilee named Nazareth, to a virgin betrothed to a man whose name was Joseph, of the house of David. And the virgin's name was Mary.

---

[1] The appellation "Son" is used of the second person of the Trinity in three distinct yet related senses in Scripture. (1) The eternal Word (John 1:1) is often referred to as "Son," and in this sense he is the *eternal Son* of the eternal Father (e.g., John 3:16–17; Gal. 4:4; Heb. 1:1–2; 1 John 4:9–10). (2) Jesus the Christ, Son of David and Son of Mary, who is the incarnate God-man, is referred to as the "Son" of God, and in this sense he is the *incarnate and historic Son* of the Father, conceived by the Holy Spirit and born of Mary (e.g., Luke 1:31–35; John 1:33–34, 49; Gal. 2:20). (3) The crucified but risen, ascended, reigning, and exalted Messiah is also referred to in a distinct way as the "Son" of God, and in this sense he is the *risen and triumphant Son* of the Father (e.g., Acts 13:32–33; Rom. 1:3-4; 1 Cor. 15:27–28; Heb. 4:14).

And he came to her and said, "Greetings, O favored one, the Lord
is with you!" But she was greatly troubled at the saying, and tried to
discern what sort of greeting this might be. And the angel said to her,
"Do not be afraid, Mary, for you have found favor with God. And
behold, you will conceive in your womb and bear a son, and you shall
call his name Jesus. He will be great and will be called the Son of
the Most High. And the Lord God will give to him the throne of his
father David, and he will reign over the house of Jacob forever, and of
his kingdom there will be no end." And Mary said to the angel, "How
will this be, since I am a virgin?" And the angel answered her, "The
Holy Spirit will come upon you, and the power of the Most High will
overshadow you; therefore the child to be born will be called holy—
the Son of God. (Luke 1:26–35)

The conception of Jesus in the Virgin Mary was unique in the
history of humankind. Not only did the Holy Spirit supernaturally
bring about conception within her apart from the involvement of any
human father, but even more remarkable was the uniting of the divine
and human natures in Jesus, such that this one would be born the son
of Mary (Luke 1:31) and the son of "his father David" (v. 32) while
also being "the Son of the Most High" (v. 32), "the Son of God" (v. 35).
That is, he would be fully human (son of Mary) while also being fully
divine (Son of the Most High). The miracle the Holy Spirit brought
to pass, then, was to conceive in Mary none other than the God-man,
the theanthropic person, Jesus Christ, son of David and Son of God.

THE NATURE OF THE KENOSIS (SELF-EMPTYING) OF THE ETERNAL SON

Given that the divine nature in Jesus was eternal and infinite while the
human nature in Jesus was created and finite, one of the questions we
ponder is just how these two natures could coexist in the one person.
Could Jesus as both fully divine and fully human be, for example,
simultaneously omnipotent, omniscient, and omnipresent—qualities of his eternal, divine nature—while also possessing a limited and
finite human power, a limited yet growing knowledge and wisdom,
and a restricted ability to be only in one place at one time—qualities of finite, human nature? It seems clear that some qualities of his

eternal, divine nature are simply incompatible with his true and genuine human nature, such that it would be impossible for him truly to live as a human if that so-called human life was also one in which he exhibited fully divine qualities such as omnipotence, omniscience, and omnipresence. In other words, would Jesus be truly and genuinely human if in his *human* experience he had limitless power, knowledge, wisdom, and spatial presence?

The crux of the answer to these questions comes in how Paul in Philippians 2:5–8 expresses the kenosis, the self-emptying, of the eternal Son as he took on human nature. Here Paul writes:

> Have this mind among yourselves, which is yours in Christ Jesus, who, though he was in the form of God, did not count equality with God a thing to be grasped, but emptied himself, by taking the form of a servant, being born in the likeness of men. And being found in human form, he humbled himself by becoming obedient to the point of death, even death on a cross.

Notice some crucial features of this important passage.

First, Paul makes clear that Christ Jesus, as the eternal Son of the Father, is fully God. He offers two expressions, each of which conveys the full deity of Christ. Paul writes that Christ existed in the "form of God" (v. 6), using the term *morphē*, which refers to the inner nature or substance of something, not its external or outward shape. So, while the English word *form* can convey merely the outward appearance of something (i.e., the shape or contour or façade of some object), not its inner reality, the Greek word *morphē* conveys just the opposite, as can be seen with Plato's "forms"—i.e., those substances of ultimate realities such as beauty, truth, justice, goodness, etc., that Plato thought existed eternally and apart from any material representation. The Greek *morphē*, then, is the inner substance or very nature of a thing, not its outer shape or appearance.

That Paul intends this understanding can be seen further in his second use of *morphē*, when he says that Jesus took the "form [*morphēn*] of a servant" (v. 7). Surely it is evident that Paul does not mean that Jesus took on merely the outer appearance of a servant, implying perhaps that though he looked like a servant, he was not in his own heart and life a true servant. Just the opposite: Jesus took on the inner substance and very nature, i.e., the form (*morphēn*), of what it means to be a servant, and that to its highest expression. As a servant, he served to the utmost, as he was obedient to the point of death, even death on the cross. So again, "form" (*morphē*, v. 6, and *morphēn*, v. 7) must mean the very nature of something, not merely its outer appearance. Therefore, Paul's point in 2:6 is clear: Jesus, being the "form of God," exists in very nature as God, with the inner divine substance that is God's alone. He is fully God since he exists "in the form [*morphē*] of God."

Paul also refers to Christ as possessing "equality [*isa*] with God" (v. 6), which likewise makes clear his full deity. Nothing is equal to God except God! As God declares of himself, through the prophet Isaiah, "I am God, and there is no other; I am God, and there is none like me" (Isa. 46:9; cf. Ex. 8:10; 15:11; Deut. 3:24; 2 Sam. 7:22; 1 Kings 8:23; Ps. 71:19; Mic. 7:18). Indeed, there is no god *other than* the one true and living God—so God is exclusively God—and there is no god *who is like* the one true and living God—so God is incomparably God. With this background in mind, Paul's declaration that Christ possesses "equality with God" is stunning. It can mean only one thing: by virtue of the fact that no one can be equal to God but God himself, Christ, who possesses equality with God, must himself be fully God. Of course, as we often find where the deity of Christ is expressed, we see hints or outright declarations that someone other than Christ likewise is God. Since he is equal to God, this means that there is another who is God, in relation to whom Christ is his equal. So, as John puts it, the Word is both "with God" and is "God" (John 1:1), and Hebrews declares that Christ is the "exact imprint" of the nature of God (Heb. 1:3). Likewise here in Philippians 2, Christ is other than the one who is God (understood as the Father, no doubt) while he is also equal to this other one who is God and so is himself fully God.

Second, when Paul writes that Christ "did not count equality with God a thing to be grasped" (Phil. 2:6), he cannot mean that Christ gave up equality with God or that he ceased being fully God. Since he is fully God, he cannot cease to be fully God. God is eternal, self-existent, immortal, and immutable, and thus he cannot cease to exist as God, nor can he fail to be fully God. Surely what Paul means is this: Christ being fully God, possessing the very nature of God and being fully equal to God in every respect, did not thereby insist on holding onto all the privileges and benefits of his position of equality with God (the Father) and thereby refuse to accept coming as a man. He did not clutch or grasp his place of equality with the Father and all that this brought to him in such a way that he would refuse the condescension and humiliation of the servant role he was being called to accept. Just how he could accept his calling to become a man while being (and remaining!) fully God, we'll explore next. But here it is crucial to see that Christ's not "grasping" equality with God cannot rightly be taken to mean that Christ gave up being God or became in any way less than fully God when he took on also a fully human nature. No, rather, he did not grasp or clutch onto the privileged position, rights, and prerogatives that his full equality with God, his Father, afforded him, in order to fulfill his calling to become fully a man who would be, amazingly, servant of all.

Third, as one who is fully God, Christ Jesus "emptied himself, by taking the form of a servant" (v. 7). The word that here is translated "emptied himself," *ekenōsen* (third aorist indicative of *kenoō*), means literally just this: that Christ "emptied himself" or "poured out himself." Note that Paul is not saying that Christ emptied something *from* himself or poured something *out of* himself, as if in so doing he became less fully God than he was before (which, as we have seen, is impossible). Rather, he emptied *himself*; he poured out *himself*. That is, *all of who Christ is* as eternal God, *all that he is* as the one who is in the form of God and is equal with God, is poured out. Christ, then, as God remains fully God. He loses nothing of his divine nature, and no divine qualities are removed from him as he pours himself out. No, Christ remains in his divine nature fully who and what he is in his existence as the eternal second person of the Trinity. He has eternally been fully God, and now in the incarnation he pours out fully who he is as God, remaining fully God as he does so.

The question then becomes just what this means—that Christ, the one who exists in the form of God (*morphē*) and as equal (*isa*) to God, pours himself out (*ekenōsen*). The answer comes, amazingly, in the three participles (particularly the first one) that follow *ekenōsen*. Christ poured himself out, *taking* the form of a servant. Yes, he pours out by taking; he empties by adding. Here, then, is a strange sort of math that envisions a subtraction by addition, an emptying by adding. What can this mean?

In brief, what this must mean is this: Christ Jesus, existing and remaining fully who he is as God, accepts his divine calling to come to earth and carry out the mission assigned him by the Father. As the eternal Son of God, who is himself the form (*morphē*, i.e., very nature) of God, he must come in the form (*morphēn*, i.e., very nature) of a servant. That is, he must come fully as a man, and as a man he must live his life and give his life as one of us. In so doing, Christ pours himself out (all of who he is) as he takes on, in addition to his full divine nature, a full human nature. Again, it is crucial to see that in the self-emptying (*ekenōsen*) of the eternal Son, Paul does not say that he poured something "out of" himself. No, absolutely not! Rather, he poured out *himself*. All of who he is as the eternal Son of the Father, as the one who is the form (*morphē*) of the Father, is poured out fully. Here, then, is no subtraction, strictly speaking. It is a "subtraction" (i.e., a pouring out, an emptying) by adding human nature to his divine nature. He came, then, to become the God-man—the one whose very divine nature took on fully the existence of a created human nature. He poured himself out by adding to himself the nature of a man, indeed, the nature of a servant *par excellence* who would give his life in obedience on the cross to fulfill the will of his Father.

Perhaps a couple of illustrations will help in seeing just how Christ could empty himself by adding something else to himself. Imagine, first, going into a new car dealership for the purpose of test-driving a brand-new car. As you are looking around the showroom floor, a salesman approaches and talks to you about several models on display. Your eye lands on a particularly bright and shiny car, brilliantly reflecting the sunlight streaming in. You ask if you can test-drive this beautiful, shiny car, and the salesman agrees. As you leave for your test-drive, you decide to drive out in the country for a bit, and in doing so you come upon some unpaved dirt roads. It so happens that this area had received torrential rains for the past several days, so these dirt roads are extremely muddy. Nonetheless, you drive this new shiny car on those muddy back roads for several miles, spinning the tires and enjoying how the car handles in these slippery conditions. Returning the car to the dealership, you pull into the lot and drive it right back onto the showroom floor—now caked all over with mud! When the salesman sees you and his car, he comes over and exclaims, "What have you done to my car?" At this you calmly reply, "I haven't taken anything away from your car; I've only added to it!" And of course, the point is correct. The beautiful shine of the car is still there. Its luster and beauty haven't been removed. But what has happened is that something else has been added to the car that prevents these qualities from being able to shine through. The beauty of the car has not been destroyed or even diminished, but that beauty has been covered over by the mud. One might even say this: the glory of the car is every bit as much present as it was previously, but this glory cannot be seen for what it is because of the covering of mud. Taking on the mud, then, had added something that results in its appearing less, while in fact it is only more.

This illustration seeks to help show just how Christ could, on the one hand, retain full deity while taking on humanity, yet, on the other hand, why it was that his deity, while fully *possessed*, could not be fully *expressed* due to his having taken on human nature. The human nature added to Christ's deity is like the mud added to the luster and brilliance of that bright and shiny car. Apart from the incarnation, there was nothing to "hide" or conceal his full deity, so it could show forth in full brilliance. But when he became also a man, he "covered" himself with a created, limited, and finite human nature. So, even though Christ is fully God in the incarnation, he cannot express the full range of his divine qualities or attributes owing to his having also taken on full human nature. While the glory of Christ's deity is still fully present and intact, the manifestation of that glory is not allowed full expression, covered as he is, in human nature. A second illustration may help further. Imagine now a great and glorious kingdom that is ruled by a strong and wealthy king. This king has every privilege one can imagine, and he possesses the finest of everything money can buy. He eats each day from the choicest cuisine, he wears the most elegant and exquisite of clothes, he is cared for by the highest educated and most skilled doctors in the land, and he is protected by an impenetrable force of royal soldiers. Yet, one day, as the king was taken on a short journey to another portion of the royal city, he passed an area he seldom had seen. Before him on the streets he observed several beggars, and he could not get these poor men out of his mind. On his return to the palace, he thought to himself, "I wonder what it is like to live life as a beggar," and he could not remove this question from his mind. So, with a determination to find out just what such a life is like, he decided to move out of the royal palace and onto some of the impoverished streets of his city. And instead of wearing the fine clothing from his wardrobe, he put on the tattered, smelly clothes of a beggar. In every way he could, he acquired the day-to-day life and limitations of a beggar. Now, having taken on the restrictions of beggarly life, when the king was hungry, although he could have called for the royal chefs to bring him a choice meal, in order to live life as a beggar he instead learned what it was like to go hungry or beg food. And when the king grew ill from the disease surrounding him, while he could have called for a highly trained doctor to attend to him, in order to live life as a beggar he accepted being sick with little if any help for his illnesses. And when insulted and mistreated by mean-spirited passersby, although he could have called for the royal guard to defend him and bring justice to bear against this cruelty, in order to live life as a beggar he accepted with no retaliation the mistreatment and insults foisted upon him.

So, while all of the qualities of his kingship were *retained* fully by this king-become-beggar, the *expression* or *manifestation* of many of the rights and privileges he had as king could not be made, since he had chosen to live life as a beggar. Or again, while the king *possessed* all of the qualities that are his as king, in taking on the life of a beggar, many of those "kingly" qualities could not be *expressed* while at the same time living fully and with integrity the life that a beggar lives.

The point is this: the king cannot live according to all the rights and privileges he knows as king *while also* living life, genuinely and authentically, as a beggar. Once he chooses to take on the life of beggar, he must necessarily accept the restriction or limitation of the *expression* of qualities, rights, and prerogatives he has as king. Although he *is* king and, hence, he continues to possess everything that is his as king, he now also *is* a beggar, so he must accept the fact that many of his kingly rights and prerogatives can no longer be utilized or expressed. Although he exists fully as king and possesses fully all the qualities that are his as king, he now has given himself fully to the task of taking on life as a beggar. And in so doing, the limitations of kingly expression are necessary. Integral life as a beggar requires these restrictions. As with the previous illustration of the mud-coated car, what this illustration of the king-turned-beggar also seeks to portray is just how Christ, on the one hand, retained full deity while taking on humanity, yet on the other hand, why it was necessary that his deity, while fully *possessed*, could not be fully *expressed* due to his having taken on human nature.

Surely the outworking of the two natures in Jesus is beyond our full comprehension. Just as with the doctrine of the Trinity in which we have in human life or experience no exact correspondence to God, who is one in essence and three in persons, so too here. We are incapable of understanding completely how one person could have two full and integral natures, especially when one of those natures is uncreated, infinite, and fully divine while the other nature is created, finite, and fully human. How it was that Christ lived fully as a man while being also fully God always has been and shall be, ultimately, a mystery. But this we know: the eternal Son of the Father, who was himself the form (*morphē*) of God and equal (*isa*) to God, took on the form (*morphēn*) of our human nature and full human servitude. As a man, he accepted finite limitations to the full expression of his infinite divine qualities, while he also possessed those divine qualities in their infinite fullness. While the fullness of these truths is beyond our complete understanding, what we are granted eyes to see, even in small measure, elicits from us awe and wonder for the greatness of the kenosis the eternal Son underwent as he became, also, fully man. As Paul describes Christ's self-emptying elsewhere, "though he was rich, yet for your sake he became poor" (2 Cor. 8:9).

THE OBEDIENCE OF THE ETERNAL SON BECOME MAN

One further element of Philippians 2:5–8 requires our attention. After explaining the kenosis itself, Paul then writes, "And being found in human form, he humbled himself by becoming obedient to the point of death, even death on a cross" (v. 8). We see here the ultimate reason or purpose of the self-emptying of the eternal Son. He became also fully a man in order that he would be able to obey the Father in going to the cross, giving his life for others. That is, while he taught much during his earthly ministry, and while he performed many good works, and while he obeyed the Father in sinless obedience every day of his life, the ultimate purpose of the Son's coming was to obey the Father to the point of death, even death on a cross. As Jesus himself said, "The Son of Man came not to be served but to serve, and to give his life as a ransom for many" (Matt. 20:28).

The point that Paul is making here has to do with the *kind* and *extent* of the obedience that this Son of the Father was required to render to fulfill his mission. Notice that Paul does not say merely that Christ, now in human form, "humbled himself by become obedient" (period)—as if now for the first time in the Son's experience did he express obedience to his Father. Surely this is not the case, since everything the Son did prior to the incarnation was an outworking of the Father's will and work for him to do. Creation, for example, was the work of the Father, brought about through the agency of the Son. There is no way to understand the biblical teaching of creation in passages such as 1 Corinthians 8:6 and Hebrews 1:1–2 without resorting to the notion of the Son's submission to the will and design of the Father. Clearly the Bible does not indicate that creation was a jointly planned work in which both Father and Son participated in exactly the same ways. No, rather, the Father created through his Son, which gives priority to the Father in the act of creation and sees the Son as subordinate in function to the Father's design and will.

Likewise, the Father's sending the Son into the world indicates that the Son not only obeyed the Father after becoming incarnate, but he obeyed the Father *in coming* to become incarnate. Jesus's words in John 6:38 are instructive: "For I have come down from heaven, not to do my own will but the will of him who sent me." For Jesus to distinguish his "own will" from "the will of him who sent" him is clear evidence that the Son followed the will of the Father in his coming. What is this if not obedience to the will and plan that the Father had designed for his Son? All of the sending language in John's Gospel bears this out. If the Son came just as much from his own plan and will as the Father's plan and will, then what does it mean that the Father sent the Son into the world? John 3:17 reads, for example, "For God did not send his Son into the world to condemn the world, but in order that the world might be saved through him." Isn't it clear from this (and many similar statements from Jesus) that (1) the Father willed to send the Son, and (2) the Father planned and purposed what the Son would—and would not—do in his coming. In short, the eternal Son submitted to and obeyed the will of his Father prior to his becoming incarnate. So, when Paul says that Christ "humbled himself by become obedient," we shouldn't stop there (for the verse doesn't), but keep reading.[2]

What did the Son suffer? He "humbled himself by becoming obedient *to the point of death, even death on a cross*" (Phil. 2:8). It

---

[2] This is precisely the mistake Millard Erickson makes in his use of this text to support the notion that the Son's obedience to the Father began and functioned only during the incarnation. He suggests that Phil. 2:8 be read to say that "Jesus actually gave up equal authority with the Father and took on an obedience to him that was not previously present." See Millard J. Erickson, *Who's Tampering with the Trinity? An Assessment of the Subordination Debate* (Grand Rapids, MI: Kregel, 2009), 120. As we've seen, it is not becoming obedient, per se, that Paul says Christ underwent, but it was the kind and extent of obedience that he accepted in the incarnation such that he became obedient to the point of death, even death on the cross.

is not the obedience, per se, that Paul is stressing—though his obedience surely is central to the whole point. The stress is on the *kind of obedience* he rendered and the *extent to which he was called to go* in obeying his Father. What *kind* of obedience is this? Here is obedience to the point of death; that is, this is obedience that accepts suffering, rejection, ridicule, and agony. Surely the Son, in eternity past, never had to embrace this kind of obedience in his relation to the Father. Although he had obeyed the Father previously as he carried out the Father's will as the agent of creation, or in coming to earth to become incarnate, never before had his obedience been rendered in a context of rejection and suffering. The kind of obedience he now rendered was new. He humbled himself to accept obedience of a kind he had not known previously. And the *extent* of his obedience is expressed as Paul continues, "to the point of death, even death on a cross." All the way to death; all the way to a cross-inflicted death—this was the extent of the obedience the Father required his Son to embrace. And he did so, fully knowing the cost to his own life and well-being. What a servant he was, indeed.

Although the eternal Son, as God the Son, obeyed the Father and fulfilled what the Father willed for the Son to do prior to the incarnation, yet it was only the God-man, the human Jesus, who could obey in this way. To obey to the point of death requires the ability to die, and for this, Jesus had to be human. To be placed on a cross required that he be in a human body, and so again, this obedience required that he be fully human. But is this not the very point Paul is making— this eternal Son who was himself in very substance God and was fully equal to God, took on our human nature precisely so that he could undergo the suffering, affliction, rejection, crucifixion, and death that he experienced, all because the Father had sent him to fulfill this saving mission? What a Savior is our Lord Jesus Christ. How amazing was his obedience, and how great was his love. May we cherish daily the beauty and agony of this eternal Son, becoming incarnate Son, all for the purpose of suffering death for our salvation.

APPLICATION

1) The single most important application from these reflections has to do with our heart responses to Jesus. Before we talk about "living like him," let's realize just what it meant for him to do what he did in coming to earth, taking on our human nature, and suffering an agonizing death on the cross to pay for our sin. Without comprehending the profundity of the purpose of the incarnation, as Paul describes it here in Philippians 2:5–9, we will inevitably trivialize what it means to "do what Jesus would do" or to "live like Jesus." How trite, until we see the heights from which he came and the depths to which he descended in coming as the suffering Servant who would bear our sin. We will belittle the magnitude of what Jesus has done if we fail to see the kind of obedience he rendered and the extent to which he was willing to go in ensuring that he fulfilled the will of his Father. The antidote to such trivializing and belittling is found in deep and prolonged meditation on the magnitude of the humble obedience and agonizing suffering of our Lord. May we take up the banner of "living like Jesus" only when we first have come to understand something more deep and profound about just what that life was like. May our minds be granted greater comprehension so that our hearts may be filled with deepened affection. Only then will we move in the direction we need to go in falling on our faces before this servitude, this obedience, that surpasses all others in all of time.

2) But having minds and hearts moved by what Christ has done, we must also recognize that Paul's opening imperative calls us to action. We should never forget that this amazing portrait of the humbling of Christ is given to illustrate what he commands believers to do. As he writes, "Have this mind among yourselves, which is yours in Christ Jesus" (Phil. 2:5). Be like Jesus, says Paul, in giving yourself in humble service to others. None of us could possibly serve in precisely the ways Christ has or to the extent that he went in rendering his obedient service. But we all are called to look to that example to inform ways in which we can, by his grace, seek to model our lives after him. This

is not works righteousness; this, rather, is worked-out righteousness. Part of what it means to be a follower of Christ is to emulate his life in the conducting of our own. May God grant us vision, grace, and strength, then, not only to grow in knowing better the greatness of his service for us but also in seeking to express greater service toward others ourselves, to the glory of our gracious and servant-hearted Lord.

DISCUSSION QUESTIONS

1) Jesus did not give up his deity, or aspects of his deity, in becoming also fully human. He was (and is!) both fully God and fully man. Given that Jesus continued to be fully God when he became also fully man, what are some things that he sometimes said, and sometimes did, during his earthly ministry that indicate he was/is fully God?

2) Amazingly, the Father sent his Son to take on our human nature in order to accomplish some things that could not have been done apart from him becoming also fully human. What are some aspects of Jesus's life and work that were central to his mission and which could only be brought about because he was, in fact, fully human?

3) The eternal Son of the Father left the highest height imaginable ("equality with God") and descended to the lowest depth possible ("even death on a cross") to bring about our salvation. Spend a few minutes meditating on and discussing what must have been true of the Son's life and experience with the Father and the Spirit prior to the incarnation. Then consider some of the elements of his life and experience in taking on the lowest position possible in obedience to the Father and out of love for sinners.

4) Recall for a moment the extent and completeness of the obedience of Christ. He never once disobeyed! And his obedience was rendered in excruciatingly difficult circumstances, at greater cost than any obedience ever rendered by any human being in all of human history. How does this help put into perspective the obedience that God calls us to render? What are some ways God calls you to obey, at times, in costly ways? How does reflecting on the extent and gravity of Christ's obedience help us when we consider ways in which we, too, are called to obey?

5) When you hear the opening imperative of Philippians 2:5, to "have this mind among yourselves, which is yours in Christ Jesus," what are some of the things the Spirit of God has helped you see that you must do to obey this command? In other words, in your life and situation, how can you stoop and serve in ways that reflect just a small part of what Christ demonstrated in his love for us?

2

EMPOWERED BY THE SPIRIT

God anointed Jesus of Nazareth with the Holy Spirit and with power. He went about doing good and healing all who were oppressed by the devil, for God was with him.

ACTS 10:38

How did Jesus live his life of obedience, resisting temptation and carrying out perfectly the will of his Father? For many evangelicals, who have been taught (correctly) that Jesus was fully God, their instinctive answer would be something along these lines: Because Jesus was fully divine and had all power available to him as God, he was able to carry out all that the Father required of him and obey the Father out of the resources of his intrinsic divine nature. In short, Jesus was perfectly obedient because he was perfectly God. Now, while it is gloriously true that Jesus was perfectly obedient, are our evangelical instincts on the right track here? Is the correct answer to the question, How did Jesus live a perfectly obedient life?, that he lived out of the power of his divine nature as one who was perfectly God?

Another question presses upon us as we consider this line of thought. If Jesus was perfectly obedient because he was perfectly God, then how can we, his followers, be called to live like him, to "follow in his steps" (1 Pet. 2:21), as Peter commands us to do? If he lived his life out of his intrinsic divine nature as God, yet we have no such divine nature and clearly are not God, is it legitimate for biblical writers to encourage—indeed, command—us to live as he did? How is it right

31

to call us to have the same mind in ourselves that was in Christ Jesus (Phil. 2:5) when we do not and cannot have the very divine nature he had to carry out the work he did—*if* in fact this is how he fulfilled what the Father sent him to do?

So, is this common evangelical intuition correct that Jesus lived his life of obedience and fulfilled the will of his Father out of the resources of his intrinsic divine nature, as God? Or does this intuition assume that Jesus lived his life of obedience out of his divine nature while not considering deeply enough the humanity of Christ also and the role his full humanity plays in how he lives his life? After all, although Jesus was (and is) fully God, from the moment of his conception in the Virgin Mary he also was (and is) fully human. The fact that Jesus is the God-man has to be considered carefully when dealing with questions of what Jesus could or could not have done and of how he was able to carry out particular activities and have particular experiences. Is it possible that the humanity of Christ has more to do with how he lived his life day by day than many of us have thought?

This serves to raise yet another key question: What dimensions of the life, ministry, mission, and work of Jesus Christ can be accounted for fully and understood rightly only when seen through the lens of his humanity? Put differently, while Christ was (and is) fully God and fully man, how do we best account for the way in which he lived his life and fulfilled his calling—by seeing him carrying this out as God, or as man, or as the God-man? I would argue that the most responsible answer biblically and theologically is the last, as the God-man, but that the emphasis must be placed on the humanity of Christ as the primary reality he expressed in his day-by-day life, ministry, and work.

The instinct in much evangelical theology, both popular and scholarly, is to stress the deity of Christ, but when it comes to the day-to-day obedience and ministry of Jesus, the New Testament instead puts greater stress, I believe, on his humanity. He came as the second Adam, the seed of Abraham, the son of David, and he lived his life as one of us. Now again, he was fully and unequivocally God, and some of the works of Jesus, in my view, displayed this deity—e.g., his forgiving of sin (Mark 2:1–12), the transfiguration of Christ (Matt. 17: 1–13; Mark 9:2–13; Luke 9:28–36), his raising of Lazarus from the dead (John 11:1–16), as the one claiming, "I am the resurrection and the life" (John 11:25), and most importantly the efficacy of his atonement whose payment for our sin, only as God, was of infinite value. These and others show forth the truth that he lived among us also as one who was fully God. But while he was fully God, and while this is crucial to understanding rightly his full identity, his life, and the fulfillment of his atoning work, the predominant reality he experienced day by day, and the predominant means by which he fulfilled his calling, was that of his genuine and full humanity. Paul captures the significance of the humanity of Christ with his assertion, "There is one Mediator between God and man, the man Christ Jesus" (1 Tim. 2:5).

In this chapter, I wish to support this claim by appeal to an astonishing biblical truth about Jesus, the Messiah: he came into this world and lived his sinless life and fulfilled his divine calling as none other than the long-awaited Spirit-anointed Messiah. That is, though he was fully God, and though he possessed the fullness of his own infinitely rich and full divine nature throughout his incarnate life on earth as he does now in his ascended life at the right hand of his Father, yet the Spirit of God rested upon his life. In other words, although he came as one who was both fully God and fully man, he also lived his life as one indwelt with and empowered by the Spirit of God. We shall here suggest that understanding Jesus as the Spirit-anointed Messiah requires that we also see his humanity as prominent in the life that he lived. Apart from his full and integral humanity, we cannot account for this central and pivotal feature that Jesus manifested, namely, that he lived his life, obeyed the Father, resisted temptation, and so fulfilled his calling all in the power of the Spirit who was upon him.

JESUS, THE SPIRIT-ANOINTED MESSIAH

One of the clearest and strongest evidences that Jesus lived his life and carried out his mission fundamentally through his humanity is that Jesus came as the Spirit-anointed Messiah. That is, Jesus was empowered by the Spirit to accomplish the work he came to do. As Gerald Hawthorne claims in his seminal study *The Presence and the Power: The Significance of the Holy Spirit in the Life and Ministry of Jesus*, the Holy Spirit's presence and work in Jesus's life is one of the most significant biblical evidences "of the genuineness of his humanity, for the significance of the Spirit in his life lies precisely in this: that the Holy Spirit was the divine power by which Jesus overcame his human limitations, rose above his human weakness, and won out over his human mortality."[1]

Now, one must ask this question: why did Jesus need the Spirit of God to indwell and empower his life? After all, he was fully God, and being fully God, certainly nothing could be added to him, for as God, he possessed already, infinitely and eternally, every quality or perfection that there is. Yet, Jesus was indwelt with the Spirit and ministered in the power of the Spirit. So, we ask: what could the Spirit of God contribute to the deity of Christ? And the answer we must give is: Nothing! As God he possesses every quality infinitely, and nothing can be added to him. So then we ask instead this question: what could the Spirit of God contribute to the *humanity* of Christ? The answer is: everything of supernatural power and enablement that he, in his human nature, would lack. The only way to make sense, then, of the fact that Jesus came in the power of the Spirit is to understand that he lived his life fundamentally as a man, and as such, he relied on the Spirit to provide the power, grace, knowledge, wisdom, direction, and enablement he needed, moment by moment and day by day, to fulfill the mission the Father sent him to accomplish.

Consider with me just a few texts that fill out and support this way of understanding Jesus:

> There shall come forth a shoot from the stump of Jesse,
>   and a branch from his roots shall bear fruit.
> And the Spirit of the LORD shall rest upon him,
>   the Spirit of wisdom and understanding,
>   the Spirit of counsel and might,

---

[1] Gerald F. Hawthorne, *The Presence and the Power: The Significance of the Holy Spirit in the Life and Ministry of Jesus* (Dallas: Word, 1991), 35.

the Spirit of knowledge and the fear of the LORD.
And his delight shall be in the fear of the LORD. (Isa. 11:1–3)

The teaching and implications of this text are massive. Ask yourself these questions: In his interactions with the Pharisees, or the crowds, or the Samaritan woman, or Nicodemus, or Peter, or the high priest, did Jesus exhibit extraordinary wisdom and understanding? Were his counsel and insight marked by discernment? Did he fear the Lord and so obey his Father from his heart every step of the way? Yes, indeed, he did. Now ask yourself this question: How would Isaiah 11:2 encourage us to account for these features that marked all of his life and ministry? The answer is that the Spirit rested on him and granted him wisdom, understanding, knowledge, discernment, strength, and resolve to fear God his Father. In other words, these qualities did not extend directly or fundamentally from his divine nature, though divine he surely was! Rather, much as the "fruit of the Spirit" of Galatians 5:22–23 is the outward evidence of the inward work of the Spirit in a believer, so too here these qualities are attributed to and accounted for by the Spirit who rested upon Jesus, empowering him to have the wisdom, understanding, and resolve to obey that he exhibited.

Consider another account from early in Luke's Gospel. After being tempted by the Devil, Luke tells us that Jesus "returned in the power of the Spirit to Galilee" (Luke 4:14), and he entered the synagogue in Nazareth, his home town, on the Sabbath. Luke writes:

The scroll of the prophet Isaiah was given to him. He unrolled the scroll and found the place where it was written,

"The Spirit of the Lord is upon me,
    because he has anointed me
    to proclaim good news to the poor.
He has sent me to proclaim liberty to the captives
    and recovering of sight to the blind,
    to set at liberty those who are oppressed,
to proclaim the year of the Lord's favor."

And he rolled up the scroll and gave it back to the attendant and sat down. And the eyes of all in the synagogue were fixed on him. And he began to say to them, "Today this Scripture has been fulfilled in your hearing." (vv. 17–21)

The fact that we are told that Jesus "opened the book and found the place where it was written" and then quotes from Isaiah 61 indicates that Jesus chose this text! Think of it: he could have turned instead to Isaiah 53, but no, he turned here. Obviously this indicates something of the significance of Jesus's identity as the Spirit-anointed Messiah. At the heart of who he is, we must see him as coming in the power of the Spirit.

Whereas the prophecy of the Spirit-anointed Messiah in Isaiah 11 focuses on Jesus's character qualities, knowledge, and wisdom, the prophecy here in Isaiah 61 focuses more directly on the Messiah's role as prophet. The Spirit will be upon him to "preach" the gospel and "proclaim" release to the captives. So when you put these two texts from Isaiah together, you realize that the role of the Spirit on the coming Messiah will be to empower his inner life and character and to fill his mind with knowledge and wisdom but also to empower the ministry he will conduct outwardly as he proclaims the message God has for him to give. Both inward character and outward conduct, then, are tied to the empowering work that the Spirit will perform on this coming anointed one of God.

Another important text is Matthew 12:28. Jesus had exorcized a demon from and healed a man who was blind and mute, but the Pharisees claimed that he had done this by the power of "Beelzebul, the prince of demons" (Matt. 12:24). Jesus gives three stinging rebukes, the last of which is this: "But if it is by the Spirit of God that I cast out demons, then the kingdom of God has come upon you" (v. 28). Of course, the main point Jesus is making is that as the Spirit-anointed one foretold over and again in the Old Testament Scriptures, he comes as the Messiah who brings in the kingdom. But don't also miss the other obvious lesson from this text. Jesus does not claim to have performed this miracle by his divine power and authority as God. Rather, he attributes the power used in this miraculous exorcism and healing to the Spirit at work in and through him.

Indeed, he accomplished these works as none other than the Spirit-anointed Messiah.[2]

Consider now Acts 10:38, a text that confirms what we've seen and provides even more reason for understanding the life and ministry of Jesus being lived and conducted as a man in the power of the Spirit. In Acts 10 Peter has been brought to Caesarea to speak the message of salvation by faith in the atoning work of the crucified and risen Jesus to Cornelius and the other Gentiles with him. After Peter explained why he had come to these Gentiles, he proceeded with his sermon about Christ. In Peter's sermon, he takes a moment to summarize the whole of Jesus's life, his moral actions, and his supernatural power with these stunning and instructive words: "You know of Jesus of Nazareth, how God anointed Him with the Holy Spirit and with power, and how He went about doing good and healing all who were oppressed by the devil, for God was with Him" (Acts 10:38 NASB).

Now, clearly Peter understood that Jesus was fully God. After all, Peter, with the other disciples, had worshiped Jesus as God's own Son when Jesus had come to them walking on the water, saving Peter from sinking as he attempted also to walk on the water toward Jesus (Matt. 14:22–33). Peter was granted revelation from the Father that Jesus was the Christ, the Son of the living God (Matt. 16:16). And Peter likewise had been present with Thomas and the other disciples when Jesus appeared in the room, and the reluctant Thomas, now seeing Jesus's pierced hands and side for himself, said to Jesus, "My Lord and my God!" (John 20:26–29). Later, Peter surely was among the company of the disciples who saw the risen Christ and worshiped him (Matt. 28:9, 17). And Peter concludes his second letter by ascribing glory both now and for eternity to the Lord and Savior Jesus Christ—an ascription appropriate only to one who is himself fully God (2 Pet. 3:18). Without question, then, Peter knows that Jesus was genuinely

---

[2] Certainly some of Jesus's miracles may have been done out of his divine nature. Indeed, it seems in John's Gospel, in particular, this may well be the case. But here Christ states specifically that the miracle performed was done in the power of the Spirit, and so we should accept this for what it says. And we'll see that Acts 10:38 likewise points generally to Jesus's healing the demon possessed through the power of the Spirit. So it seems reasonable to conclude that the norm for accounting for the miracles that Jesus did is not through an appeal to his divine nature, per se, but rather by an appeal to the power of the Spirit who indwelt him.

and fully God—which is what makes this statement in Acts 10:38 all the more remarkable.

In his sermon to Cornelius, when Peter brings to mind the life and ministry of Jesus, and just how Jesus lived his life and carried out the will of the Father who sent him, Peter does not refer to the deity of Christ per se but rather to his humanity, filled with the Holy Spirit. He comments to Cornelius on two broad areas about Jesus's life and ministry: (1) Jesus went about "doing good," a reference to the moral obedience and uprightness of Jesus throughout the whole of his life; and (2) Jesus went about "healing all who were oppressed by the devil," a reference to the miraculous works of Jesus in healings and other signs and wonders, opposing the power of the Devil and of sickness and disease. So, Jesus lived a life of exemplary and perfect obedience, doing all the good the Father commanded him to do, and he lived a life exhibiting miraculous powers over the Devil, sickness, and disease.

But how did Jesus live this perfectly obedient life and accomplish these miraculous works? Peter's answer from this verse is this: "*God anointed Jesus of Nazareth with the Holy Spirit and with power*," and he did these good things and performed these miracles because "God was *with* him" (Acts 10:38). Clearly, the template Peter had in mind in understanding and accounting for the life and ministry of Jesus was this: although Jesus was fully God, he was, more precisely, the God-man. That is, he was God in human flesh, so he was simultaneously fully God and fully man. And as a man, Jesus was the Christ, the long-awaited Messiah of Israel, a man born in the line of David, anointed and empowered by the Spirit to live out his life and carry out his mission. Was Jesus also fully God? Indeed, he was. But it was "the man Christ Jesus," filled with the Spirit, whom Peter sees here as living in complete obedience to his Father, exercising supernatural power over demons and diseases and fulfilling the mission the Father sent him to accomplish. Jesus the man, filled with the Holy Spirit and with power, lived this life marked by perfect obedience and supernatural empowerment.

Notice one further point here, if you would. Can you imagine that the similarity in language between Acts 10:38 ("God anointed Jesus of Nazareth with the *Holy Spirit* and with *power*") and Acts 1:8 ("You will receive *power* when the *Holy Spirit* has come upon you") is accidental or merely coincidental? I highly doubt it. It seems rather that Luke's point would be this: the very power by which Jesus lived his life and carried out his mission (Acts 10:38) is now ours since the Holy Spirit who was on him is given to us, his followers (Acts 1:8). What incredible new-covenant reality is now ours in Christ, by the indwelling Spirit! The long-awaited internalization of the Spirit (Ezek. 36:27) is granted only as that Spirit first dwelt in Jesus, empowering his life and obedience, only then to be granted to Jesus's followers. This side of the empty tomb and Pentecost, we, too, may live lives marked by that same supernatural Spirit-wrought empowerment for obedience and faithfulness. The very resource of Holy Spirit empowerment granted to Jesus for his life of obedience and faithfulness to the Father is now granted to Jesus's disciples as they carry forward the message of Christ, living lives of obedience to Christ, all in the power of the Spirit.

Something even further about the extent of the Spirit's work in and through Jesus can be seen from Isaiah 42:1–4:

> Behold my servant, whom I uphold,
>   my chosen, in whom my soul delights;
> I have put my Spirit upon him;
>   he will bring forth justice to the nations.
> He will not cry aloud or lift up his voice,
>   or make it heard in the street;
> a bruised reed he will not break,
>   and a faintly burning wick he will not quench;
> he will faithfully bring forth justice.
> He will not grow faint or be discouraged
>   till he has established justice in the earth;
>   and the coastlands wait for his law.

Evangelicals rightly understand this first of Isaiah's Servant Songs to be fulfilled in Christ. As Jesus comes in the power of the Spirit, he comes to accomplish what has been established for him to do. And here the main point we saw from Isaiah 11 continues, viz., that the ability the Servant will have to accomplish these marvelous works, from possessing a character that is gentle and kind to his relentless work to bring about justice, is power granted him by the Spirit. In other words, once again we see that it is not the divine nature of the Messiah per se that is the source of the power he uses to live his humble life and accomplish great feats, but it is the power of the Spirit, who rests upon him, that he draws upon.

This text is complicated in a certain way, as are many Old Testament texts that announce the coming of the Messiah. The complication is simply this: not all of what is prophesied to happen when the Servant (Messiah) comes actually takes place during the life and ministry of Jesus Christ on earth. Much like in Isaiah 9:6–7, where we do not now see the peace on earth that the Davidic King was said to bring to pass in his coming, so too here there are elements that seem not to be fulfilled as Jesus arrives born of Mary. Can we rightly say that he brought forth "justice to the nations" or that he "established justice in the earth" during his first coming? Certainly it is true that Christ did all the work necessary for these elements of the prophecy to be realized one day in their fullness, but this side of the "not yet," we await the establishing of global justice that this text announces. This surely is one of the big surprises for the disciples of Jesus who were granted eyes to see that he was in fact the long-awaited Messiah. As the Messiah, they expected that he would bring in his kingdom, that peace and righteousness would prevail over all the earth. They expected the enemies of Israel to be vanquished and God's own people delivered from all external rule and oppression. Why did they have these expectations? They had them because they had read their Old Testament Scriptures and seen that these things will take place when the Messiah comes!

So we have learned, as John the Baptist had to learn (see Matt. 11:1–6), that some of what is promised concerning the Messiah actually did take place during the life and ministry of Jesus, but much of the fullness of his prophesied messianic work awaits his second coming. Will Messiah bring peace and righteousness to earth? Yes, but although by his death and resurrection in his first coming he accomplished the work necessary to bring this to pass, the consummation of the fullness of this promise awaits his second coming. We live in the "already" of what has, in preliminary and partial manner, been fulfilled thus far, while we await the "not yet" of the full consummation of the fulfillment of these promises.

Now let's return to our main point, that the Servant who will come will live his humble life and accomplish his glorious work in the power of the Spirit, as Isaiah 42:1–4 announces. One more observation is needed in light of what we have just seen of the "already" and the "not yet." When one looks at what the Servant, Jesus, will do in the power of the Spirit, this text refers fundamentally to elements of his work that will take place in his second coming, not his first. True enough, elements of verses 2 and 3 are fulfilled in his first coming; e.g., he does come quietly, as it were, with a humility, meekness, and servant-heartedness that fit the descriptions of these verses. But, the larger teaching of bringing forth justice to the nations and establishing justice on the earth awaits his second coming.

And all of this gives rise to this realization: this promised Servant will accomplish the work of his second coming, just as he did the work of his first coming, *in the power of the Spirit*. So here we have evidence not only that Jesus lived his life and conducted his ministry in his first coming in the power of the Spirit (as we saw in Isa. 11:1–3), but also that the Spirit will remain on him and empower the work that he has yet to accomplish in his second coming. Indeed, the incarnate Jesus, since he is forever human from the moment of his conception in the womb of Mary, forever has the Spirit upon him working through him to accomplish the work the Father has given him to do.

This same idea can be seen from Isaiah 11:1–4. We looked earlier at the description of this prophesied Davidic descendant who would manifest wisdom and knowledge and discernment and the fear of the Lord through the power of the Spirit (vv. 1–3). And clearly all of these features were fulfilled in the person of Jesus Christ in his first coming. But verse 4 indicates more of what the Messiah will do, and these additional features simply do not fit the first coming of Christ. Isaiah writes:

> But with righteousness he shall judge the poor,
>   and decide with equity for the meek of the earth;
> and he shall strike the earth with the rod of his mouth,
>   and with the breath of his lips he shall kill the wicked.

When did Jesus in his first coming vindicate the poor and bring justice to the meek? When did he take up his role as judge over the earth? And, in particular, when did he strike the earth with the rod of his mouth and slay the wicked with the breath of his lips? We might recall here what John says about Jesus's (first) coming in John 3:17: "For God did not send his Son into the world to condemn the world, but in order that the world might be saved through him." Surely the day is coming when this very same Jesus will come again, and when he comes he will indeed strike the earth with the rod of his mouth and slay the wicked (see Rev. 19:11ff.), but this did not happen in his first coming. His first coming was for the salvation of the nations; his second coming will bring to those nations his fierce and relentless judgment. So, again, we are faced with a prophecy of the Spirit upon Jesus who will strengthen him to do what we now know will take place only in his second coming, not his first. The Spirit, then, must continue to reside upon the crucified and risen Jesus to empower him to accomplish what yet must be done to fulfill all that has been promised.

A small but meaningful confirmation of this line of thought is found in Acts 1:1–2. Luke writes, "In the first book, O Theophilus, I have dealt with all that Jesus began to do and teach, until the day when he was taken up, after he had given commands through the Holy Spirit to the apostles whom he had chosen." One can read over this little but significant item and easily miss its contribution to this discussion. In all likelihood, the "commands" that Luke refers to in verse 2 are the commands of the Great Commission that Jesus gave to his disciples following his resurrection and prior to his ascension. But there is one detail that Luke could easily have left out, but his inclusion of it instructs us about the risen Christ. Luke indicates that

Jesus gave these orders, the teaching of the Great Commission, to his disciples "through the Holy Spirit." In other words, the risen Christ continues to have the Spirit upon him, and it is the Spirit upon him who continues to empower him to carry out the work he is called upon to do.

Although Jesus was the God-man such that he possessed a fully divine as well as a fully human nature, it seems clear from the study we've undertaken to conclude that the bulk of Jesus's day-to-day living occurred as he fulfilled his calling, obeyed the Father, resisted temptation, and performed his confirmatory miracles, fundamentally as a man empowered by the Spirit. He lived his life as one of us. He accepted the limitations of his humanity and relied upon the guidance the Father would give him and the power the Spirit would provide him to live day by day in perfect obedience to the Father.

Again, one must come to terms with the significance of the repeated biblical teaching that Jesus, the Messiah sent from God, would be marked by having the Spirit upon him. But why would he need the Spirit since he possessed already the infinitely full and complete divine nature? What can the Spirit of God add to the deity of Christ? He can add nothing, since the deity of Christ is infinitely full and perfect. But what can the Spirit of God add to the humanity of Christ? He can add everything of supernatural enablement! Yes, Jesus, the Spirit-anointed Messiah, lived his life as a man, accepting the limitations of his human existence, and relied on the Spirit to do in and through him what he could not do in his human nature. His identity, then, as the Spirit-anointed Messiah is fundamentally that of a man empowered by the Spirit to carry out what he was called upon to do.

APPLICATION

1) The most pressing application from this understanding of Jesus is that the life of obedience and faithfulness that Jesus lived can genuinely and rightly be set forward as an example of how we, too, should live, precisely because the very resources Jesus used to live his obedient life are resources given also to all of us who trust and follow

him. Think of it: he relied on the Word of God, and we too have that same divinely inspired Word. He relied on prayer, and we too have full access to the throne of grace through the entrance that Jesus has established on our behalf. And importantly, he relied on the Spirit, who empowered him to do the good things he did and to carry out the supernatural works God called him to do, and we too now have that very same Spirit. Has it ever occurred to you how privileged we are to live this side of Pentecost? How amazing it is that the very same Spirit who was on Jesus has now been given to all who follow Jesus. So Peter is vindicated in his command to follow in Jesus's steps (1 Pet. 2:21ff.), since, as Jesus lived his life as a man in the power of the Spirit, we too as human beings are granted the same supernatural power to live faithfully in our own lives.

2) We also see something of the humility of the Son here that should lead us to worship and to awe and wonder. Although Jesus possessed fully his divine nature, and through his divine nature he had access to infinite divine wisdom and power, he accepted instead the role of living life in dependence upon what the Spirit would provide for him for the purpose of living life as one of us, as a man with all the limitations that such a life involves. Rather than drawing upon the infinite resource of his divine nature, he prayed for help and trusted both his Father and the Spirit to bring to him what he needed. He accepted our life as his own, and in this he showed amazing humility. Marvel at this humble Son, who, though fully God, accepted living life as a man, dependent upon the Spirit each day of his life. Marvel and then worship.

3) Finally, when Jesus took on our human nature and accepted his dependence on the Spirit, it seems that he accepted this as his way of life forever, from that moment forward without end. Since he would always be the God-man, and since he would always in his person have his human nature joined to his divine nature, he always would need the Spirit to empower him in his humanity for all that he would continue to be called on to do as the Messiah. When he became also human,

he did so forever. And when he became also human, he became forever dependent on the Spirit. How amazing to think that the eternal Son of the Father was willing to go to this extent to demonstrate his honor of the Father's will and his love for us sinful humans, that he would become a man dependent upon the Spirit forever. What love, what condescension, and what honor and thanks is owed to this great Savior.

DISCUSSION QUESTIONS

1) The church has long held that the *imitatio Christus* is an important, even essential, part of our lives as Christians; that is, we are called to imitate Christ in how we live our lives. What are some of the main passages where we are commanded, as followers of Christ, to live like him? And what are some of the specific ways our speech, actions, attitudes, and behavior should reflect Christ?

2) In his obedience to the Father, Christ relied on resources given to him in his humanity that now, this side of Pentecost, are also given to us, his followers. Christ relied on the Word of God, on prayer, on the community of faith, and on the presence and power of the Holy Spirit. Consider the ways in which Christ himself relied on these resources and how they were manifested in the way he lived his life.

3) The resources given to Christ for his obedience are now given also to us. For each of these—Scripture, prayer, community of faith, Holy Spirit empowerment—consider just how well you are doing in making use of these God-given means. How are you making use of the resource of Scripture? How might you grow in taking greater advantage of this resource to strengthen your life, your obedience, your resisting temptation, your faithfulness? And how are you making use of the resource of prayer? Of the community of faith? Of the gift and power of the Holy Spirit?

4) How might the Spirit in particular want to work more in and through us to see Christ's character formed and Christ's conduct exhibited? Consider one of the main roles of the Spirit revealed to us in Scripture, that he moved biblical writers to write just what they did in the pages of the Bible. Reflect on

2 Peter 1:20–21 in considering what the Spirit wants to do to form us more to be like Christ.

5) Consider the character qualities referred to as the "fruit of the Spirit" in Galatians 5:22–23. Reflect first on how these qualities were exhibited in Christ's own life and dealings with people. Then consider how the Spirit might seek to see these qualities increase in your life and in your dealings with others. That is, how would the Spirit have you grow in love, in joy, in peace, and in the other qualities mentioned?

3

INCREASING IN WISDOM

And the child grew and became strong, filled with wisdom. And the favor of God was upon him. . . . And Jesus increased in wisdom and in stature and in favor with God and man.

LUKE 2:40, 52

It really is quite remarkable that in all of the Gospels, only one incident of Jesus's childhood years is recorded for us. Luke 2:41–51 provides for us the fascinating account of Jesus in Jerusalem, taken there by his parents at twelve years of age for the Feast of the Passover.

SETTING

We're told very little about what took place during the days that Jesus and his family were in Jerusalem for this feast, but we are told what happened when his parents and others left Jerusalem to travel back to Nazareth. Jesus remained in Jerusalem and was found with the Pharisees and teachers of the law at the temple. Luke records for us this summary statement of Jesus's time with those learned men at the temple in Jerusalem: "After three days they found him in the temple, sitting among the teachers, listening to them and asking them questions. And all who heard him were amazed at his understanding and his answers" (Luke 2:46–47).

Mary and Joseph were not as interested in the conversations that Jesus had had with these teachers of the law. Having made the effort to come back to Jerusalem to claim their son, they were dismayed over the fact that Jesus had decided to stay behind instead of traveling with them back to Nazareth. Jesus's mother said to him, "Son, why

have you treated us so? Behold, your father and I have been search-
ing for you in great distress" (v. 48). Then Jesus gave this surprising
and remarkable response to his mother. He asked her, "Why were
you looking for me? Did you not know that I must be in my Father's
house?" (v. 49). Although neither Mary nor Joseph could understand
at that time just what Jesus meant by this (v. 50), it is clear that Jesus
understood as a twelve-year-old boy that his true Father was not his
legal, human father, Joseph, but was instead his heavenly Father—the
Father who had sent him into the world and had given him the mission he had come to do. He knew who his true Father was, and he
had come to do the will of his true and heavenly Father. Here in the
temple, in his Father's house, he was engaged in conversations that
were preparing him for what was yet to come a number of years later,
conversations that also revealed much about just who Jesus was as a
twelve-year-old boy.

SOURCE OF JESUS'S WISDOM

This remarkable account of Jesus's interaction with the teachers of the
law in Jerusalem raises a very important question for our understanding of Jesus: just what accounts for the remarkable questions, answers,
and understanding that Jesus evidenced in his conversations with these
learned men? I think that many of us in the conservative evangelical
tradition would have a ready answer. We would say, instinctively, the
reason Jesus had such remarkable understanding of the law was that
he was God in human flesh. After all, we might think, those Pharisees
and teachers of the law didn't understand who they were dealing with.
If they had only known the truth, that this twelve-year-old boy was
none other than the incarnate God-man, they would have understood
that his wisdom came from his being God. So, given that he was God
in human flesh, we reason, even as a twelve-year-old boy Jesus was
able to astonish the greatest teachers in Israel.

I believe that this evangelical intuition, as we might call it, that
Jesus's wisdom and understanding are accounted for by appeal to his
deity, is not the answer that Luke, the Gospel writer, wishes us to

see. Consider Luke 2:40 and 52, which function as bookends around this account of Jesus's childhood visit to Jerusalem. Luke 2:40 records that "the child grew and became strong, filled with wisdom. And the favor of God was upon him." And Luke 2:52 reads, "And Jesus increased in wisdom and in stature and in favor with God and man." Amazingly, what both of these verses indicate is that Jesus's wisdom is not a function of his divine nature but is the expression of his *growth as a human being*.

One compelling reason for seeing this wisdom as his growing human wisdom is that Luke speaks of Jesus as growing in wisdom while also becoming stronger physically (increasing "in wisdom and in stature"). So the wisdom that Jesus has, evidently, is a growing wisdom that parallels or accompanies his growth physically. And from this observation it should be clear that the wisdom of which Luke speaks cannot be the wisdom of Jesus's divine nature. The divine nature, I take it, is not susceptible to growing in wisdom. The wisdom of his divine nature cannot rightly be spoken of as growing or increasing since it is, like all God's essential attributes, infinitely full and perfect. As God, Jesus in his divine nature is infinitely wise. As such he is both omniscient and omnisapient. He knows everything that can be known, and his use and appropriation of that knowledge is perfect. Hence the wisdom that Jesus had in his divine nature was not subject either to growth or to decline. But here we see Luke speaking of a wisdom in Jesus that grows and increases. Must this not be, then, the wisdom of his human nature? As a boy, Jesus learned, no doubt, through the instruction of his parents, and from the teaching of the rabbis in his hometown of Nazareth, and through his own diligent reading of God's Word. It was by these means that he grew and increased in wisdom. We conclude, then, that for Jesus to grow in wisdom, as Luke stresses at both sides of this childhood account, it surely indicates a growth that takes place in the human nature of Jesus.

One other very important clue that Luke has in mind the growing human wisdom of Jesus is a brief but illuminating statement that he gives to us in verse 40. After he observes that Jesus as a child grew and became strong, filled with wisdom, he then comments, "And the favor of God was upon him." Although we cannot be completely sure what favor Luke has in mind, one thing is clear: Jesus's growth in every way—physically, emotionally, spiritually, and intellectually—was a result of the Father's favor shown to his Son, now a little boy growing into adulthood. Surely this was the Father's favor in providing for his Son all that he would need, to grow and develop to fulfill the calling the Father had given to him. And among the ways in which he needed to grow—indeed one of the most important ways that he did grow as a boy and a young man—was his growth in understanding the truths of the Word of God.

But then one might inquire: What might be the substance of this "favor of God" upon him that would result in Jesus's growth in wisdom? Though Luke does not tell us, a number of other Scriptures seem to lead us in this direction for our answer: this favor of God would most likely be the gift of the Spirit, whom the Father poured out upon his Son, now in human flesh, granting him insight and increased understanding of God's Word and will as he grew. It seems reasonable, in any case, to understand Luke's reference to the favor the Father placed upon his Son to be the Spirit, who came upon him at his conception. Luke has already told us that the miracle of Jesus's incarnation happened as the Spirit came upon Mary, and the power of the Most High overshadowed her so that the Holy One born of her would be called the "Son of God." And again here, it seems reasonable to conclude that the Spirit's role was not only to come upon Mary but also to come upon Jesus and indwell him at his very conception.

One clue that Luke intends us to understand the Spirit coming upon Jesus at his conception is the juxtaposition he gives in Luke 1:35 of the *Holy* Spirit coming upon Mary so that the child born of her is himself *holy*. Luke likely has in mind here not only the conception of Jesus as sinless but also the conception of Jesus as indwelt by the Holy Spirit. After all, if John the Baptist, the forerunner of Messiah, was indwelt by the Spirit while yet in his mother's womb (Luke 1:15), how much more important for the Messiah himself to have the indwelling Spirit from the very beginning of his life. In any case, this childhood account of Jesus in Luke 2 does indicate that God's favor was upon

Jesus, causing him to grow in wisdom. And it seems reasonable to understand that the favor shown him here was the gift of the Spirit, who indwelt Jesus as he grew, enabling him, among other things, to increase in wisdom.

Further support for the Spirit's work in Jesus to grant him the wisdom he needed comes from Isaiah 11:1–3. Since we considered this text in the last chapter, we'll just review the most relevant aspects here. Isaiah announces, as you recall, the coming of one from the stump of Jesse, David's father. And the description he gives us of this coming son of David focuses upon the role of the Spirit in his life. Isaiah says of him, "And the Spirit of the LORD shall rest upon him, the Spirit of wisdom and understanding, the Spirit of counsel and might, the Spirit of knowledge and the fear of the LORD" (v. 2). What is particularly noteworthy for our purposes here is the element of Isaiah's prophecy that connects the *wisdom* of this coming son of David with the *Spirit*, who would rest upon him. He will be wise but not wise of himself or wise of his own divine nature per se. Rather, he will be wise because the Spirit of the Lord will rest upon him, "the Spirit of wisdom and understanding."

Isaiah's prophecy tells us, then, that this coming son of David would display a wisdom that is brought about within him through the indwelling Spirit of God. And isn't it interesting that the first record we have of the wisdom of Jesus is in this childhood account recorded for us in Luke 2? Long before his baptism and the public ministry he conducted in his early thirties, Jesus exhibited wisdom in his interaction with the teachers of the law in Jerusalem at the age of twelve. Isaiah's prophecy, then, surely lends support to the understanding that the wisdom Jesus demonstrated, even at this early age, was none other than the wisdom wrought in him by the Spirit of God.

As we think of the boy Jesus with the teachers of the law in the temple, not only did he have wisdom internally, but he spoke that wisdom to those in his hearing. You might recall that Isaiah 61:1–3 connects the indwelling Spirit on the Messiah with his role of proclaiming the Word of God. As Jesus spoke with these learned men in Jerusalem, it seems most likely that the Spirit of God not only granted him wisdom in his understanding but also empowered what he said to those in his hearing so that they marveled at what he said. The teachers of the law with Jesus on that day in the temple were amazed at his understanding through the questions he asked and the knowledge he exhibited. How would Luke want us to interpret the remarkable nature of Jesus's understanding of the Word of God and his articulation of that Word to teachers of the law at the temple? The favor of God was upon him as the Spirit of God granted him supernatural wisdom, understanding, and articulation of those truths, speaking forth what the Word of God had declared in the power of the Spirit.

One more question comes to mind as one contemplates the young boy Jesus growing in wisdom by the power of the Spirit: just what did the Spirit do to bring about this increase and growth of wisdom in Jesus as he grew from childhood to adolescence to adulthood? How did the Spirit bring about this growth? It stands to reason that the Spirit of God did with Jesus what he seeks to do with all of us in whom he dwells: he illumined the Word of God to Jesus's mind and cultivated that Word in his heart as Jesus read, studied, heard, and was taught that precious, Spirit-inspired Word. We all know, of course, that the adult Jesus exhibited an extraordinary knowledge of the Old Testament Scriptures, evidenced in his dealings with various people as recorded in the Gospel accounts. There's no question but that he knew his Bible well. But how did he come to know the Bible as he did? How did he have such mastery of its content and ability to bring appropriate texts to mind when needed? Was his knowledge of the Bible automatic? Did he "just know" all of it due to his being fully God?

Again, Luke's affirmations that Jesus increased in wisdom lead us to think this is not the right answer. Yes, he surely was God, and in his divine nature he knows the Scriptures perfectly, since he knows all things perfectly. But if Jesus "increased in wisdom," then his knowledge was not out of his divine nature per se. Rather, his human nature had to acquire the knowledge and wisdom that he later evidenced, whether at the age of twelve or thirty.

So again, how did Jesus acquire such knowledge and wisdom so that even at the age of twelve he could converse with the most learned men of Israel? Here is what must be the core of our answer: Jesus was what might be thought of as the Psalm 1 prototype. He truly loved the law of the Lord and meditated upon it day and night. Because of this, he was like a tree planted by rivers of water that yields its fruit in season; its leaf did not wither, and in whatever he did he prospered. Out of his love for the law, he learned and mastered that law, and the Spirit within him illumined his mind and enflamed his heart to long to know it better and better as he grew.

There is a reason why Psalm 1 is the first psalm of the Psalter. It not only describes the wise and the wicked as general categories of human beings; it describes in particular the Wise One, whose wisdom surpassed all others as he grew in wisdom through the power of the Spirit. The Spirit, then, worked in the mind and the heart of the young boy Jesus to grant him a hunger for the Word of God and insight into that Word as he was taught and as he meditated upon it in quiet study and reflection.

Given the Spirit's work in Jesus as a boy growing up to grant him increasing wisdom, this would surely include the increasing understanding he would have of Scripture. So if this is the case, imagine this with me: there must have been a day in the life of the young boy Jesus when he was meditating through the psalms and came upon Psalm 22. As he reflected on the weightiness of the suffering described there, the despair and agony depicted, the Holy Spirit illumined Jesus's mind to understand that the one spoken of in the psalm, forsaken by God and given over to unimaginable torment, was none other than himself. We know, of course, that Jesus knew that Psalm 22 applied to him, for he quoted its opening line from the cross. When did he come to know that this psalm was about him? Either he simply knew this automatically, as it were, since he was God. Or, as being argued here, as a man in whom the Spirit dwelt, the Spirit chose the time and place to illumine his young mind to see what he had not seen before and to be caught up in the reality that this psalm, with its suffering and rejection, was about him.

Imagine the day when Jesus was reading through and meditating upon the prophet Isaiah. When he came to chapter 53, the Spirit must have opened his mind and heart to understand from this text that he was in fact the suffering servant of whom Isaiah wrote. He would be the one who would bear the sins of many. He would be the one crushed by his Father, the one through whose work the Father would be able to justify the many. Imagine the growing wisdom of Jesus as he read and studied God's Word. The Spirit of the Lord within him would grant him increasing understanding not only of the truth of that Word but also of his identity as the Son of God, the suffering servant, the one who came into this world to give his life a ransom for many. When Jesus tells his parents in Jerusalem that he must be in his Father's house and about his Father's business, we realize that at merely twelve years old he knew who he was and the work he had come to accomplish.

Marvel, then, at these small but profound observations recorded for us in Luke's Gospel, that Jesus "grew and became strong, filled with wisdom. And the favor of God was upon him" (2:40), and that Jesus "increased in wisdom and in stature and in favor with God and man" (v. 52). How instructive these observations are in telling us of the humanity of Jesus. He lived his life as one of us, learning what he didn't previously know and depending on the Spirit to grant him wisdom from on high. His dependence on the Spirit would have been as great as his devotion to the Scriptures. With diligence and joy, he poured over those inspired texts, and the Spirit gave him increasing depth of understanding and discernment into their meanings.

How well did he need to know those Scriptures to be prepared for the public ministry the Father had designed for him? Perhaps the fact that he commenced that public ministry at age thirty gives us part of the answer. For three decades the Spirit worked within Jesus, instructing him and bringing him yet greater and greater insight, until finally the day came when he was ready to face the Devil, the Pharisees, the demons, and his disciples, all with the Word of God deeply enmeshed in his soul. Marvel that Jesus, our Lord and Savior, grew in wisdom. And ask yourself, what does that say about how we should live our lives?

APPLICATION

1) One lesson we learn from this early account of Jesus, the Spirit-anointed Messiah even in his youth, is how important the connection is between the Spirit and the Word. The Spirit came upon Jesus in part to illumine his mind to understand and then speak forth the truth of God's revealed Word. In order for Jesus to fulfill his mission, he had to learn the Word of God, and to learn this Word well and rightly he needed the Spirit within to illumine his mind and heart. Another way to think of this observation is this: it would have been impossible for Jesus to accomplish the work the Father had given him to do were it not for the knowledge and wisdom he acquired, by the Spirit's enablement, from the Word of God. We dare not, then, separate Word and Spirit as if we can fulfill God's work and live in a manner pleasing to God with one but not the other. No, Spirit and Word are inseparable in God's economy, and Jesus bears glorious testimony to this truth. May we learn from Jesus that yielding to the Spirit and devotion to the Word are necessary companions.

2) Another application from this brief account of Jesus's boyhood experience in Jerusalem is that Jesus understood the importance of engaging in biblical and theological discussion and learning. We don't know the exact content of the discussion that took place, but we know that Jesus stayed deliberately to speak with the teachers of the law in Jerusalem. The obvious topic of conversation would have been the Word of God. And while it must have been the case that Jesus saw the opportunity to raise in their minds questions from Torah that would help them understand better the coming of the Messiah, there is no indication that Jesus had a confrontation with them. Hence his purpose was genuine discussion for greater illumination and understanding of God's Word. It even stands to reason that part of Jesus's purpose in staying behind was to learn from these master teachers more of the Law of the Lord, which he loved so dearly. After all, Jesus learned much through the whole of his upbringing. And here he had an opportunity to sit at the feet of some of the most learned men in all

of Israel. His purposes would have involved both giving to them and gaining from them in their discussion over the law of the Lord.

So often we consider theological discussion a waste of time or, worse, divisive and hurtful. But, oh, how our understanding of theological discussion needs to change. We should see such discussions of weighty biblical truths as opportunities for growth in our understanding of God and his Word, along with subsequent growth in our application of that Word to our lives and ministries. As with every other good thing in life, theological discussion can deteriorate into something harmful. But it need not and should not. Rather it can be the very thing that God would call us to do for the sake of being refined in our understanding and encouraged in our faith.

3) Another remarkable lesson from this account relates to the humility Jesus exhibited. After Jesus's parents found him in the temple, and after learning that the teachers of the law were amazed at his questions and his understanding, and, even more, after they heard Jesus say that he had to be in his Father's house—with all of this, they might have thought that Jesus was past the need for their parenting and really should be left to himself. But instead his parents instructed him to come with them back to Nazareth. After all, he was merely twelve years old. And then we read this in Luke 2:51: "And he went down with them and came to Nazareth and was submissive to them." It really is nothing short of astonishing that this same Jesus, who clearly understood his identity as the Son of the heavenly Father, would choose to put himself under the authority of his human parents. His submission to them indicated his commitment to follow the law of the Lord that commanded children to obey their parents, to honor their father and mother. Though he was God in human flesh, and though the Spirit of God within him had enabled him to understand his identity as the long-awaited Messiah of Israel, he yielded in submission to his human parents.

The humility shown in Jesus is remarkable and instructive. It shows, on the one hand, that submission is in fact a positive quality. The culture in which we live views submission of any kind negatively.

But here Luke's point is to commend Jesus for his willingness to obey and to submit to his parents. Submission, then, is a good thing. But even more importantly we see that submission can be rendered by one who is in no way inferior or subordinate in essence to the one to whom he submits. Jesus, the God-man, submitted to his parents. In no respect does this indicate Jesus's supposed inferiority to his parents. Just the opposite is the case—Jesus was superior to his parents, for he was both God and man together. But nonetheless he had come for the purpose of fulfilling his role as the Spirit-anointed Messiah, and this involved submitting to his human parents.

May we marvel, then, at Jesus, who displayed such godly humility as manifested in his submission to his parents at the very point of life when it had become clear to him that he was the incarnate God-man, the Messiah of Israel. May we learn that submission is never rightly understood as a demonstration of the inferiority of the submissive one or the superiority of the one in authority. Rather, may we understand that God's design for all of us is to render willing submission in many relationships in life. In so doing we express something of the quality we see here in Jesus, one that we should rightly seek to emulate.

DISCUSSION QUESTIONS

1) Luke 2:40 and 52 tell us that the young Jesus increased in and was filled with wisdom. What does this tell us about Jesus's childhood? And how does this help us understand better the genuineness of the humanity of Christ?

2) How could Jesus grow in wisdom since he was fully God as well as fully human? Since the deity of Christ is infinitely wise and cannot grow in wisdom, and since Jesus possessed the divine nature completely in its infinite fullness, what does this tell us about the relationship of the divine nature in Jesus to his human nature?

3) Reflect on the subject matter of the twelve-year-old Jesus in his conversation with the teachers of the law in the temple. They spoke of Old Testament teaching, and these teachers were astonished at what Jesus said and the questions he raised. What does this tell us about Jesus's attitude toward the Word

of God and his commitment to learn what that Word taught? If we truly want to be more like Jesus, what does this tell us about our attitude toward and involvement with the Bible?

4) What is the relation between the Spirit and the Word in Scripture? Do they act independently or autonomously? Or does the Spirit work through the Word and the Word through the power of the Spirit? Which answer is true in relation to Christ and how he lived his life?

5) Since Spirit and Word work together, how might this better help us understand how Jesus was filled with the Spirit, and how we, too, should be filled with the Spirit? In considering this question, meditate upon these two texts together: Ephesians 5:18 and Colossians 3:16a. These are parallel texts, which can be seen by the fact that the same basic outcomes (seen in Eph. 5:19–20 and Col. 3:16b) flow from the different imperatives of each of these verses. And, when seen together, this couplet of passages can help us understand more of what it means to be filled with the Spirit.

4

GROWING IN FAITH

*In the days of his flesh, Jesus offered up prayers and supplications,
with loud cries and tears, to him who was able to save him from death,
and he was heard because of his reverence. Although he was a son, he
learned obedience through what he suffered. And being made perfect,
he became the source of eternal salvation to all who obey him.*

HEBREWS 5:7-9

For many Christians, when they consider Jesus's spiritual life, they imagine that it must have been somewhat fixed and static. After all, since he was the Son of God, since he possessed fully the divine nature, and since he lived a sinless life, there could not be any sense in which Jesus "grew" in his spiritual life, so it is thought. Rather, his life with the Father must have been one of static and unbroken fullness, with no sense of growth even possible.

At one level, this intuition is true. Since Jesus never sinned, and since he always did the will of his Father, he always enjoyed the unbroken approval of the Father and lived in intimate and unbroken union with his Father. As John 15:10 declares, Jesus abided in his Father's love because he always kept his Father's commandments.

But there is another sense in which Jesus's spiritual life was anything but static. In fact, his was the most dynamic and growing of all spiritual lives possible precisely because he lived from his heart this life of unbroken obedience and submission to the Father's will. In other words, Jesus's life of perfect obedience did not render his spiritual life a static experience devoid of any growth. Just the opposite: precisely because he obeyed the Father perfectly, including in times of opposition, agony, affliction, and suffering, this perfect obedience actually resulted in the most profound and radical growth in his spiritual life—a growth of faith greater than anyone has ever experienced.

LEARNING OBEDIENCE AND BEING MADE PERFECT

Consider with me Hebrews 5:8–9. This brief text contains some intriguing phrases in particular that are deeply instructive as we reflect on their implications for understanding the life of faith that Jesus lived. Hebrews here says of Jesus that he "learned obedience through what he suffered," and also that, "being made perfect," he was able to save those who obey him (v. 8). Now, I submit to you that anyone whose mental conception of Jesus is that he was fully divine (which, of course, he was!) will have a difficult time accounting for this kind of language. After all, if Christ lived his life fundamentally out of his divine nature—a nature that is infinitely perfect and incapable of learning anything—then what does Hebrews mean here? But if Christ lived his life fundamentally (not exclusively) out of his human nature, then the concepts of his learning what he did not know and "being made" what he was not previously can begin to make sense. So what do these statements in this text tell us about Jesus?

Our first statement, in Hebrews 5:8, tells us that though he was a son, Jesus "learned obedience through what he suffered." It is important to note that the previous verse indicates that this was his experience during the incarnation and so would not have been true of him eternally. It was "in the days of his flesh," i.e., his human, incarnate life on earth, that "Jesus offered up prayers and supplications, with loud cries and tears, to him who was able to save him from death, and he was heard because of his reverence" (Heb. 5:7). So, we understand that the experience Hebrews is describing here must be of the human Jesus and would not be true—indeed, could not be true—of this Son strictly in his divine nature, which was the case prior to the incarnation. Jesus as a human offered up prayers with loud cries and tears, and Jesus as a human learned obedience through what he suffered.

Another indication that Hebrews 5:7 is contemplating Jesus in his humanity is the mere fact that he offered up prayers and supplications. In his divine nature Jesus had infinite power and exhaustive knowledge, so his prayers and supplications indicate one of the many expressions of the limitations he encountered as an integral human being. Why offer supplications—requests—if you already know everything, including the answer to your own prayers? And furthermore, why cry out with loud cries and tears to another who can save you when you have unrestricted power over anyone who might threaten you? Clearly, Jesus felt strongly his need for divine assistance, and he understood how fully dependent he was on what must be provided to him by another. So, again, verse 7 helps us see that Hebrews is pondering Jesus's human experience, one in which he felt deeply his vulnerability, his weakness, his ignorance of some aspects of the future, and the need to look to another for guidance and protection.

Having established that this was the human experience of Jesus, we inquire next just what this fascinating teaching of Hebrews 5:8 means, that Jesus "learned obedience through what he suffered." In order to get at this, let's first consider two possibilities that prove, upon examination, not to be plausible. First, some might think that this phrase refers to the fact that Jesus learned to obey his Father for the first time in the incarnation. In other words, Jesus as the eternal Son of the Father, fully equal to the Father in his divine nature, never did or could have obeyed the Father prior to the incarnation, since such obedience would indicate some sense in which he was lesser than the Father. Only in the incarnation, so it is argued, is the concept of obedience appropriate; only as he took on human nature did he experience for the first time what it was to obey his Father. After quoting Hebrews 5:8, Millard Erickson writes, "This [passage] suggests that obedience was something that he learned" and that such "obedience was perhaps something unusual or unexpected for a son."[1]

---

[1] Millard J. Erickson, *Who's Tampering with the Trinity? An Assessment of the Subordination Debate* (Grand Rapids, MI: Kregel, 2009), 121.

There are two reasons for questioning this interpretation: (1) Jesus's own teaching about his relationship with the Father prior to the incarnation suggests his obedience to the Father, indeed, his submission to the Father's will, in coming to earth to become incarnate. Jesus said, "For I have come down from heaven, not to do my own will but the will of him who sent me" (John 6:38), and again, "I came [from God] not of my own accord, but he sent me" (John 8:42). It seems clear that if in Jesus's coming, he did not do his own will but the will of his Father who sent him, and if he did not come on his own accord but came as the Father sent him, then he acted in obedience to fulfill the will of his Father in his coming to earth. It was not his own will per se that led him to come, but the will of the Father who sent him. We certainly do not want to be in a position where we conclude that the Son was forced to come by his Father; obviously he chose gladly and freely to come. The point is that his choosing to come was a choice to submit to his Father's will. So, the obedience of the Son took place in eternity past, prior to the incarnation, as the Son chose to do the will of his Father in coming to take on our human nature.

2) Hebrews does not merely say that Jesus "learned obedience." Rather, the statement reads that he "learned obedience *through what he suffered*." So, the point is not that he learned to obey for the first time ever in his experience, but that he learned to obey within this particular context of suffering, agony, affliction, and opposition. The Son's obedience in eternity past was true obedience, but it was not an obedience forged in the fires of suffering. In the incarnation, the Son's obedience was unlike the obedience he had rendered previously. This "incarnate obedience," we might call it, was rendered often within the context of opposition and affliction, with the result, often, that his obedience was the cause of much further suffering. In other words, he knew that as he obeyed the Father, he was inviting only greater opposition and was putting himself in a place of increased suffering. Obedience per se was not new; rather, this *kind* of obedience was indeed new.[2]

---

[2] A similar line of thought applies to Phil. 2:8, where Paul states of the incarnate Son, "And being found in human form, he humbled himself by becoming obedient to the point of death, even death on

Another possible explanation of what Hebrews means when it says, "he learned obedience through what he suffered" can be eliminated summarily. Some might think that Jesus finally learned to obey the Father, having disobeyed him many times previously. In other words, the point is that Jesus finally "got it." He finally learned that he needed to obey rather than disobey. While this may be our experience (at least, we hope we learn to obey when we have disobeyed many times previously!), it simply cannot be what this text means. Just a few verses earlier, Hebrews declares of Jesus that he was tempted in every respect as we are, "yet without sin" (4:15). Obviously it follows that since Jesus never sinned, Jesus never disobeyed the Father. No, it simply cannot be the case that Hebrews means here that a previously disobedient Jesus finally learned to obey.

If these proposals cannot be the meaning of Hebrews 5:8, just what is this text saying? Allow me to offer two suggestions.

1) Although Jesus was a Son, and as a Son he deserved only honor, allegiance, respect, and adoration from those with whom he dealt, he encountered from these very people much hatred and opposition. He was afflicted, scorned, ridiculed, and rejected by many people in many ways. And within this context of suffering, Jesus knew that his obedience to the Father and the Father's will would mean only continued and intensified suffering. Yet, despite the suffering he knew he would receive, he resisted the temptation to avoid suffering and to turn away from the Father's will and instead resolutely obeyed the Father every step of the way, no matter how hard things were. Indeed, Jesus learned to obey the Father's every directive and command without fail or compromise (e.g., John 8:28–29), even at great cost, even though he knew his obedience would bring to him only intensified pain, affliction, rejection, suffering, and ultimately an agonizing death from those who opposed him.

---

a cross." Again here, the statement is not merely that Christ "humbled himself by becoming obedient" (period), as if he had never previously been obedient to the Father. As argued above, his very coming to earth to become incarnate was an act of obedience and submission to the will of his Father (e.g, John 6:38; 8:42). Paul's assertion here, rather, points to the nature and extent of the obedience of the Son— an obedience that was so great, so extensive, so complete, so sacrificial, so other-serving, that it was an obedience "to the point of death, even death on a cross." As above, the Son's rendering obedience per se was not new; rather, this *kind* of obedience to this *extent* was indeed new.

2) Jesus obeyed the Father in the context of suffering, knowing that his obedience would only aggravate the intensity of that suffering, but Hebrews is saying more than this. And this gets at the heart of the notion that Jesus's spiritual life was anything but static, and that Jesus in fact grew in his relationship with the Father and grew in faith every step of the way as he obeyed the Father in the midst of suffering. Notice that Hebrews does not declare (merely), "Although he was a son, he obeyed the Father in the midst of what he suffered," as remarkable as that would be. But read carefully that this text says something additional. It declares more amazingly, "Although he was a son, he *learned* obedience through what he suffered." In what sense, then, did Jesus learn to obey?

Must it not be that Hebrews is indicating that Jesus learned to obey the Father through the whole of his life with an obedience that was rendered in increasingly difficult situations as he grew and developed? As the Son learned to obey the Father in earlier times of "lighter" divine demands upon him and consequent "lighter" suffering—lighter, that is, in comparison both to the divine demands and the suffering he would encounter in the end, as he obeyed the Father in going to the cross—these earlier experiences of faith in the Father's provision, protection, and direction prepared him for the greater acts of obedience he would need to render as he got nearer to the time of the cross. In other words, those earlier "obediences," we might call them, under circumstances with lighter suffering and affliction, were prescribed by the Father as the training program necessary to prepare Jesus for the later and much harder obediences that were to come. He *learned* to obey increasingly difficult divine demands with their accompanying increasingly difficult opposition and affliction through the whole of his life, which prepared him for the greatest of all divine demands upon him and the greatest attending suffering he would or could ever experience. In this sense, then, the difficulties and afflictions Jesus experienced through the whole of his life were planned by his Father in order to prepare Jesus for the greater—and indeed, greatest!—acts of faith he would need to render to complete the Father's mission for his Son.

Consider a couple of indicators that seem to warrant this reading of Hebrews 5:8. First, look at what Hebrews had just told us in verse 7. We read there not only that Jesus offered up prayers and supplications to the Father throughout his life ("in the days of his flesh") but that he did so "with loud cries and tears." Unless we trivialize what this is declaring, would we not have to conclude that the situations this verse points to are ones in which Jesus experienced agonizing hardship and difficulty in his endeavor to obey the Father? Does this not indicate that Jesus's trust in the Father and his dependence on what the Father alone would provide him was hard fought and won? Throughout his life he fought to believe and fought to obey and fought in prayer as he hoped in what the Father would provide. To put this point differently, Jesus's faith and obedience during these times of testing, in which he offered supplications with loud cries and tears, were not experiences of an easy walk of faith or effortless acts of obedience. Jesus's obedience was not automatic, as though his divine nature simply eliminated any real struggle to believe or effort to obey. No, in his human nature, Jesus fought for faith and struggled to obey; otherwise the reality that Hebrews 5:7 describes is turned into theatrics and rendered disingenuous. The inclusion of "with loud cries and tears" tells us, then, of the reality of the struggle Jesus endured as he trusted and obeyed his Father, praying earnestly for what he needed to fulfill the Father's will.

Additionally, Jesus's life of fighting to believe and obey is confirmed when we consider afresh his experience in the garden of Gethsemane. Matthew (26:36–46) and Mark (14:32–42) both tell us that Jesus prayed three time in the garden that the Father would remove the cup from him. Three times, also, Jesus declared that despite this deep and strong desire to avoid the agony of the cross, he longed even more to do the will of his Father, not his own will. Luke's rendering (22:39–46) adds the poignant comment, "And being in an agony he prayed more earnestly; and his sweat became like great drops of blood falling down to the ground" (v. 44). It is simply impossible to think deeply about these accounts and draw the conclusion that since Jesus was God, and since it was impossible for him to sin, his obedience here in the garden was both automatic and easy. Everything in these passages cries for the opposite conclusion. His obedience was anything but automatic and easy; it was rather extremely difficult and hard fought. Praying three times, as Jesus did, indicates the deep struggle to embrace in that place and time the Father's will that he go to the cross. This battle for belief in the goodness and rightness of the Father's will was not over quickly or easily. If there had been some resolution immediately upon praying the first time, why pray a second time, and then a third?

Furthermore, Jesus's comment to his disciples, "My soul is very sorrowful, even to death; remain here, and watch with me" (Matt. 26:38), indicates an agony of soul that we probably cannot even fathom. And his request that his disciples pray with him and for him also shows his earnestness of heart as he faced the impending suffering of the cross. All of these factors point to the same conclusion: Jesus felt deeply and agonizingly the weight of the suffering he was being called to endure; he longed to avoid it if at all possible, and so he prayed fervently that God would strengthen him to do it, leading him, then, to embrace fully what the Father had sent him to do.

Let me draw two conclusions from this discussion. First, Jesus's struggle to believe and obey the Father was real! Oh, my, how horrible to the meaning of these texts, and how dishonoring to our Savior, to think or propose that because he was fully God, his obedience here and elsewhere in his life was easy and automatic. Nothing could be further from the truth. His obedience here was difficult, painful, agonizing, even tortuous, and he felt deeply and in prolonged fashion the struggle to believe and obey his Father.

Second, given the fact that this was the *greatest* act of obedience he rendered, requiring the *deepest* commitment of faith and hope in his Father, in light of the *severest* of all suffering he was about to encounter on the cross, does it not stand to reason, then, that the Father had prepared Jesus for this moment? Can we not now see that all the previous tests of his faith, the divine demands that he followed and the sufferings that he experienced, were preparatory and strengthening for his obeying the Father in the garden? So here's an interesting question: Could Jesus have obeyed the Father and gone to the cross to die for our sins when he was twelve years old? Could he have done so at the outset of his ministry, at age thirty? Or did the Father know just when his Son's faith would be strengthened sufficiently so that at this time he was able to engage the fight and withstand the temptation and declare in the end, "Not my will, but yours, be done" (Luke 22:42)? Indeed, Jesus learned obedience from the things he suffered. That is, he learned to obey increasingly difficult demands of the Father, preparing him for this hardest of all demands—going to the cross. Could he have faced this Gethsemane challenge successfully at the ages of twelve or thirty? I think the answer is no. As remarkable as his obedience was each step along the way, all of these experiences were meant to build his faith and strengthen his character so that he could, in the end, succeed in fulfilling the will of the Father in choosing to endure the agony of the cross for the remission of our sins.

This discussion leads naturally to a consideration of the second striking and surprising description of Christ that Hebrews uses. After we have been told that Jesus "learned obedience through what he suffered," Hebrews says, "And being made perfect, he became the source of eternal salvation to all who obey him" (5:9). Made perfect? And this is being said of the Son of the Father? What can this mean, and how can this be? In light of what we've seen, it should become apparent what is being declared here. As the sinless Son of God, Jesus was nothing other than perfect in terms of his righteous character and faithful obedience before the Father. He never moved from sinfulness to sinlessness, as we are in the process of doing by God's grace. No, he was sinlessly perfect. So, in what sense can Hebrews declare that Jesus was "made perfect"?

The term used in Hebrews 5:9 for "perfect" refers to bringing to completion or moving to a planned or desired end. The English words *complete* or *mature* can also translate this Greek term. The issue for Jesus was not one of moving toward sinless perfection, for he was always sinlessly perfect. The issue rather was one of character formation and faith maturity, such that he would be able, in the end, to obey the Father's most difficult demand upon him and go to the cross. I admit that for many believers this concept is a hard one to appropriate—character formation for Jesus? And faith maturity for the sinless Son of God? But clearly Hebrews is speaking about some manner in which Jesus was made perfect, mature, or complete in a way that he was not previously. And as we've seen already, this cannot refer to some fundamental change in Christ's human nature from some degree of sinfulness to sinlessness. Rather, this has to be a kind of maturity that takes place within the fully sinless human nature of Jesus. And given the fact that Hebrews declares that Jesus was "made perfect" immediately after telling us that Jesus had "learned obedience through what he suffered," it stands to reason that the perfection or maturity of 5:9 is the outcome of his having learned obedience from what he suffered.

The perfection, maturity, or completion accomplished in Jesus, then, was the strengthening of his character and faith to the point where he would be able to accept fully the will of the Father to go to the cross. His "being made perfect" is precisely about his growth in faith and his strengthening of character and resolve through his lifetime of testings and sufferings so that he was fully mature and able, through prayer and divine enablement, to accomplish the work the Father had sent him to do. And as Hebrews 5:9 reminds us, it is only because he was so perfected, it was only through the pathway of this process of the maturity of his character and faith, that Jesus was able to be the "source of eternal salvation to all who obey him."

Much was at stake, then, not only in Jesus's going to the cross but in his having lived the kind of life he did—learning to obey increasingly difficult demands of the Father, enduring suffering such that his faith and character were strengthened—in order that when the moment of greatest testing came, he would embrace his Father's will and give himself over to die for our sins. Praise be to God for Jesus's death on the cross for our sins! In addition, praise be to God for Jesus's life of deepening obedience and growing faith that prepared him to accept, in the end, the ultimate purpose for which the Father had sent him into the world. So, let us rejoice that Jesus "died for our sins" (1 Cor. 15:3). But let us remember that this happened only because it is also true that Jesus became "obedient to the point of death, even death on a cross" (Phil. 2:8). The life he lived prepared the way for the death he died. Praise be to a Savior, the only Savior of sinners, who gave himself with resolve and passion to the will of his Father, "learning obedience" and "being made perfect" through the trials and testings of life, that he might be able, in the end, to save all who believe and follow him.

APPLICATION

1) There are no "little obediences." Every opportunity given us by God, either to obey or to disobey, is an opportunity for that character formation and strengthening of faith that can prepare us for the greater challenges of faith God has in mind for us in the future. Clearly, this was true for Jesus. He had to undergo the trials, testings, sufferings, and afflictions the Father designed for him in order to strengthen and prepare him for the greatest test of his faith imaginable—to accept the Father's will in going to the cross.

Jesus's training ground of tested faith is the same kind of training that the Father designs for us. When we see this, it transforms how we think about the "little" acts of obedience or disobedience we face repeatedly throughout each day. We can think of those "little obediences" as of minor or trivial importance, whereas, seen rightly, they are divinely ordained means to "perfect" us, to enable us to "learn obedience" so that through these tests of faith, we are matured and strengthened in our character. We have no idea what greater opportunities of kingdom work or faith expression might await us in the future if only we are obedient now in smaller ways, preparing us for these bigger challenges that God, in his mercy, may bring our way. May we learn from Jesus that every obedience matters. May we obey in the smaller things that we may be prepared for the larger. May we understand the role that faith testing plays in the preparation for what God may have designed for us in the future. May we be more and more like Jesus in his resolve to obey and obey and obey, no matter the cost.

2) Suffering, affliction, trials, testing—these are gifts granted to us by God for our growth, the necessary paving stones along the pathway

that leads to our fullness of character and joy. Just as Jesus's life of faith and obedience transforms our understanding of the importance of the little obediences of life, so does Jesus's pathway of growth transform how we think of suffering. There is nothing accidental in suffering. The God who declares "the end from the beginning" (Isa. 46:10) and works all things after "the counsel of his will" (Eph. 1:11) is fully in control of every situation of pain or suffering that we encounter.

Oddly, some Christians seem instinctively to want to push away suffering. They think it best to keep suffering at arm's length. But not only is this a mistake biblically and theologically; it is a huge mistake spiritually and practically. Oh, what strength there is to know that God controls and ordains suffering precisely because only through such suffering do we grow in the ways God intends for us, strengthening us for what he has in store for the future. Jesus was prepared to face the greatest challenge of his life—the greatest challenge anyone ever could face, period!—only because his Father had graciously taken him through the training ground of suffering by which he "learned obedience" step by step by step. May God help us to see the divine wisdom in ordained suffering and the goodness of God in the trials of our lives, and may we grow through these, as Jesus did, in ways that strengthen our character and bring greater glory to God.

3) The life of faith, of growing faith and strengthened character, is one that involves a fight for faith and enduring through difficulties. This life of faith is never lived on auto-pilot; it is never a life of passivity and ease; it isn't something done to us without our full and active participation. These glimpses we've seen of Jesus—who offered prayers and supplications through loud crying and tears, who prayed three times in the garden of Gethsemane for the cup to be removed—give evidence to the active, war-like nature of the life of faith. If anyone might be thought to have lived life on auto-pilot, it would be Jesus. After all, along with his true and full humanity, he was fully God; and although he had the nature of a man, his human nature was totally sinless. You would think such a person (unlike any of us!) could coast. To have a divine nature and a sinless human nature would seem to

make obedience easy. Well, look again at Jesus. What you see is a man who labored to obey, who agonized in the testings the Father designed for him, who fought through the trials of life to maintain his integrity and obedience before his Father.

In light of this, it should be certain that we who are not God, we who do not have sinless natures, will find it necessary also to fight for faith and labor for obedience. Yes, as with any and every act of faith and obedience, we affirm with Paul, it is "not I, but the grace of God" with me. Only by God's sustaining and empowering grace can we obey. But this divine enablement does not replace our responsibility to fight and labor. Rather, such divine enablement activates our resolve and puts in motion the fight of faith necessary to obey.

In the end, may we be more like Jesus. May we count every obedience significant and see each as a stepping stone toward the greater opportunities God has for us. May we embrace suffering as one of the means God uses to bring about this growth in faith and strengthening of character we need so very much. And may we resolve to fight every step of the way, by God's rich and unfailing grace, to see God's purposes in and through our lives fulfilled through our increasing faith and obedience before him.

DISCUSSION QUESTIONS

1) Isn't it astonishing that Jesus, the sinless God-man (Heb. 4:15), nonetheless "learned obedience from the things that he suffered" (Heb. 5:8)? How does this help us to appreciate more the life that Jesus lived, the temptations he encountered, and the afflictions he endured? How is your attitude toward Jesus affected from understanding this about him?

2) If God used suffering and affliction in Jesus's life to bring about maturity, does it not stand to reason that he has ordained also to bring affliction into our lives for the same purpose? Reflect on your recent past and consider some of the difficulties you've encountered and the sufferings you've undergone. Can you now see these as God-designed means to afford you the opportunity to trust and grow? What can you learn from your responses to these past experiences that can help you face future God-designed affliction?

3) Consider more specifically just how suffering in our lives can produce character change and maturity of faith. Think about some very clear examples of affliction you've encountered and consider the specific benefits that came to you, or could have come to you, from these distresses.

4) There are no "little" obediences, precisely because every opportunity to obey is one in which we may either grow in our trust in God or turn from him. In light of this, consider some of the "little" ways you have obeyed or disobeyed in recent weeks. Can you see in these small opportunities ways in which your heart can be strengthened by obedience, or how it can be rendered more cold and indifferent from disobedience? How does this affect your attitude about these opportunities to obey what God has commanded?

5) Jesus's obedience was not automatic. It was not easy for him to resist temptation and to obey. He fought every step of the way in his struggle to obey what the Father commanded him to do. How does this understanding of Jesus help us as we face struggles and obstacles in our fight to obey the good and wise commands of God?

5

RESISTING TEMPTATION

For we do not have a high priest who is unable to sympathize with our weaknesses, but one who in every respect has been tempted as we are, yet without sin.

HEBREWS 4:15

The theological question that will direct our reflections in this chapter is as follows: How can one account rightly for the reality of the genuine temptations of Jesus if one holds also that the one tempted, viz., the theanthropic person who was both fully God and fully man, was himself genuinely impeccable and as such, could not sin?[1] Of course, the problem raised by this question would disappear immediately if we denied either of the assertions for which the question seeks resolution. That is, if we deny the genuine reality of Christ's temptations, there is no longer an apparent problem in holding to his genuine impeccability. Or if we deny Christ's genuine impeccability, there would seem to be a more natural accounting for the possibility, at least, of Christ's being genuinely tempted. The problem of this chapter, then, is framed by two assertions that most in the history of theology have wanted to maintain:[2] (1) Christ was genuinely tempted, and (2) Christ was genuinely impeccable. How can both be true?

---

[1] As traditionally defined, "impeccability" asserts of Christ not merely that he *did not sin* (which is true) but more strongly that he *could not sin*. As impeccable, Christ not only was *posse non peccare* (able not to sin) but more importantly was *non posse peccare* (not able to sin).

[2] M. E. Osterhaven clearly overstates the historical acceptance of the doctrine of Christ's impeccability when he says, "The teaching that Jesus Christ was sinless (impeccable) . . . has been a universal conviction of the Christian church." "Sinlessness of Christ," in Evangelical Dictionary of Theology, ed. Walter A. Elwell (Grand Rapids, MI: Baker, 1984), 1018. Nonetheless, he rightly points to the fact that even advocates of the most notorious Christological heresies in the early church typically did not deny the sinlessness of Christ even if they were less certain about his impeccability.

It is clear from the outset that the humanity of Christ is central to how we deal with this question and the related issues, since it is clear that Jesus's humanity must be involved in his temptations in a way that his deity could not be. James informs us of something very important as we consider the temptations of Christ: "God cannot be tempted by evil" (James 1:13). But Jesus was tempted. In fact, Hebrews tells us that he was "tempted as we are, yet without sin" (Heb. 4:15). So the temptations of Jesus relate directly to his humanity, to be sure. But we also must take full account of the fact that in addition to being fully human, Jesus was fully God. As such, it has seemed to most theologians, myself included, that as God—better, as the God-man—he was impeccable; i.e., he could not sin. So, how do we account for the reality of the genuine temptations of Jesus if one holds also that the one tempted was himself genuinely impeccable and as such could not sin? And how does our understanding of the deity and the humanity of Christ relate to our accounting for his impeccability, his temptability, and his sinlessness?

SAMPLING OF EVANGELICAL TREATMENTS

Perhaps a bit of background might help from some who have addressed this issue. Louis Berkhof treats this problem briefly, presenting the issue but then offering only the most teasing and indecisive of responses. After discussing several biblical texts that affirm clearly that Christ experienced real and regular temptations throughout his ministry, Berkhof continues, "We may not detract from the reality of the temptations of Jesus as the last Adam, however difficult it may be to conceive of one who could not sin as being tempted."[3] He then offers some suggested resolutions without committing himself to any of them, concluding: "But in spite of all this the problem remains, How was it possible that one who *in concreto*, that is, as He was actually constituted, could not sin nor even have an inclination to sin, nevertheless be subject to real temptation?"[4] End of discussion.

Herman Bavinck's treatment is more satisfying. He affirms that

---

[3] Louis Berkhof, *Systematic Theology* (London: Banner of Truth, 1939), 338.
[4] Ibid.

Scripture teaches both the real temptations of Christ and his real sinlessness. Concerning the latter, Bavinck asserts that Scripture "prompts us to recognize in Christ, not just an empirical sinlessness, but a necessary sinlessness as well."[5] In other words, it is not merely a matter of historical record that Christ did not sin; more to the point, it was logically impossible for him to sin. So, Christ was genuinely tempted while he was genuinely impeccable. What supports the Christian belief in Christ's impeccability? Bavinck understands two equally problematic implications of denying impeccability and saying, as did Arius, Pelagius, and some medieval nominalists, that Christ in principle could have sinned. It would be the case that either "God himself would have to be able to sin—which is blasphemy—or the union between the divine and the human nature is considered breakable and in fact denied."[6]

But how then can we understand the temptations of Christ? Bavinck suggests a distinction between the innate holiness of the divine nature of the person of Christ and the ethical holiness of his human nature. In brief, the innate holiness of his divine nature renders Christ genuinely impeccable, while the ethical holiness of his human nature renders Christ open to temptation, struggle, obedience, and growth. He concludes that in Christ's temptations "he was bound, fighting as he went, to remain faithful; the inability to sin (*non posse peccare*) was not a matter of coercion but ethical in nature and therefore had to be manifested in an ethical manner."[7]

William G. T. Shedd has an extended treatment of this question, devoting a full chapter of his *Dogmatic Theology* to "Christ's Impeccability."[8] Shedd accounts for the impeccability of Christ by asserting the superiority of the will of his divine nature over the will of his human nature. Obviously affirming the dyothelitism of the sixth ecumenical council, Constantinople III in 680, he writes, "An impec-

---

[5] Herman Bavinck, *Reformed Dogmatics*, vol. 3: *Sin and Salvation in Christ*, ed. John Bolt, trans. John Vriend (Grand Rapids, MI: Baker, 2006), 314.
[6] Ibid. In support of this claim, Bavinck cites Augustine, *Enchiridion*, 36, 40–41; and Peter Lombard, *Sentences*, III, dist. 12.
[7] Bavinck, *Reformed Dogmatics*, 314.
[8] William G. T. Shedd, *Dogmatic Theology*, vol. 2, 2nd ed. (Nashville: Thomas Nelson, repr. 1980), 330–49.

cable will is one that is so mighty in its self-determination to good that it cannot be conquered by any temptation to evil, however great."[9] Christ's divine nature, then, is impeccable since the will of this divine nature cannot be tempted toward evil, much less to do evil. Christ's human nature and will, however, are peccable. But even though Christ's human will could sin, his divine will strengthened the human will such that the human will, so divinely empowered, could not sin. On its own, the human nature could sin, but in union with the divine nature, Christ could not sin. Shedd provides a helpful analogy:

> Consequently, what might be done by the human nature if *alone*, and by itself, cannot be done by it in this *union* with omnipotent holiness. An iron wire by itself can be bent and broken in a man's hand; but when the wire is welded into an iron bar, it can no longer be so bent and broken. . . . A mere man can be overcome by temptation, but a God-man cannot be. . . . Consequently, Christ while having a peccable human *nature* in his constitution, was an impeccable *person*. Impeccability characterizes the God-man as a totality, while peccability is a property of his humanity.[10]

Furthermore, Shedd holds that the main reason that Christ's human nature, when in union with the divine nature, could not sin (though it could sin on its own), is that the holiness of the divine nature is such that it could not tolerate sin. But if the human nature were able to sin when joined to the divine nature, this would inevitably compromise the holiness of the divine nature itself—which is both unthinkable and impossible. In such a case, "the guilt would not be confined to the human nature" but the divine nature also would be stained.[11] Since this cannot occur to the immutably holy divine nature, once the union of human and divine natures has occurred, the human nature is rendered impeccable by virtue of its union to the impeccable and overpowering divine nature.

But, then, how could the impeccable Christ be truly tempted? Shedd distinguishes between the *constitutional susceptibility* of

---

[9] Ibid., 330.
[10] Ibid., 333 (emphasis original).
[11] Ibid., 334.

Christ's human nature, which was vulnerable to weakness and limitation and open to both physical and mental temptations, and the *human will* of Christ, which now as joined to the divine nature and will, was not able to yield to whatever temptations he faced. So, while the temptations were strongly felt and experienced by a human constitution fully susceptible to temptation, he remained unable to sin by virtue of the divine will's supernatural empowerment that would not allow the human will to sin. Shedd explains, "Those temptations were very strong, but if the self-determination of his holy will was stronger than they, then they could not induce him to sin, and he would be impeccable. And yet plainly he would be temptable."[12]

Thomas Morris and Gerald O'Collins have offered variations of a proposed understanding that would account for Christ's impeccability and the genuineness of his temptations. According to this proposal, Christ could be both impeccable and genuinely tempted so long as he did not know that he was impeccable. Morris explains the idea this way:

> We have said that it seems to be a conceptual truth that, in some sense, temptation requires the possibility of sinning. On reflection, we can see that it is the *epistemic* possibility of sinning rather than a broadly logical, or metaphysical, or even physical possibility that is conceptually linked to temptation. . . . Jesus could be tempted to sin just in case it was epistemically possible for him that he sin.[13]

Similarly, O'Collins states that "Jesus could be truly tempted and tested, provided that he did not know that he could not sin." If Christ were impeccable and knew himself to be so, then the biblical accounts of his struggle and agony in temptation would simply have been "a performance put on for the edification of others."[14]

As a sample of a contrary perspective we may consider the pro-

---

[12] Ibid., 336.

[13] Thomas Morris, *The Logic of God Incarnate* (1986; repr. Eugene, OR: Wipf & Stock, 2001), 147–48.

[14] Gerald O'Collins, *Christology* (Oxford: Oxford University Press, 1995), 271. Klaus Issler seems also to follow the Morris-O'Collins proposal since he discusses the issue of Christ's impeccability and temptation, citing approvingly the contributions of these two scholars. "Jesus' Example: Prototype of the Dependent, Spirit-Filled Life," in *Jesus in Trinitarian Perspective: An Introductory Christology*, ed. Klaus Issler and Fred Sanders (Nashville: Broadman, 2007), 215–16.

posal offered by Millard Erickson. For Erickson, Scripture teaches clearly that Christ *did not sin* and that God *cannot sin*. But this does not logically require, he insists, that Christ could not have sinned. Hebrews 4:15 would seem to indicate that although Christ never did sin, he must have been able to sin, Erickson reasons. According to this text, Christ "in every respect has been tempted as we are, yet without sin." But if he was tempted in every respect, must this not include the fact that he could have yielded to temptation? Erickson writes, "The thrust of the passage is that he is able to intercede for us because he has completely identified with us; this seems to imply that his temptation included not only the whole range of sin, but the real possibility of sinning."[15] Erickson considers Morris's view, discussed above, and dismisses it as inadequate. I would concur.

But, hypothetically, what would have been involved in the event that Christ had sinned? Since God cannot sin, the deity of Christ could not have been involved in the act of sin that Christ, in this hypothetical scenario, would have committed. But how not, since the divine and human natures are joined in the one person of Jesus Christ in the incarnation? Erickson suggests, "At the very brink of the decision to sin, where that decision had not yet taken place, but the Father knew it was about to be made, the Second Person of the Trinity would have left the human nature of Jesus, dissolving the incarnation."[16] So, apparently Erickson considers as hypothetically possible one of the horns of the dilemma that Bavinck had wanted to avoid. Indeed, the union of the divine and human natures would be, in this case, breakable, in order to protect the divine nature from involvement in sin. And also interesting is the observation that Erickson and Shedd seem to agree that in the *union* of the divine and human natures in the person of Christ, Christ could not sin. Both accept the position that if Christ sinned in his person, i.e., in the union of his human and divine natures, this immoral act would necessarily implicate the divine

---

[15] Millard J. Erickson, *The Word Became Flesh: A Contemporary Incarnational Christology* (Grand Rapids, MI: Baker, 1991), 562.
[16] Ibid., 563. Another who argues similarly to Erickson is Thomas P. Flint, "The Possibilities of Incarnation: Some Radical Molinist Suggestions," *RS* 37 (2001): 307–320.

nature in Jesus. Where Shedd argues from this that the divine nature overpowers the otherwise peccable human will rendering the theanthropic person of Christ impeccable, Erickson argues that if Christ were about to commit an act of sin, in this hypothetical situation the divine nature would have first separated from the human nature in Christ so that the sin committed would be done by the human nature alone and not involve the holy and impeccable divine nature.

AN ALTERNATE PROPOSAL

For some time now, I have considered another possible way of dealing with this issue, one that flows from a strong sense that Christ should be understood to have lived his life of sinless obedience as a man, anointed and empowered by the Spirit to live his life and carry out his calling, obedient to the end.[17] Essentially this proposal runs as follows: Jesus was genuinely impeccable owing to the fact that in the incarnation it was none other than the immutable and eternally holy second person of the Trinity who joined to himself a full human nature. Nonetheless this impeccability of his person did not render his temptations inauthentic or his struggles disingenuous. How so? Jesus resisted these temptations and in every way obeyed his Father, not by recourse to his divine nature but through the resources provided to him in his full humanity. In short, this proposal suggests that coming to terms with the distinction between why it was that Christ *could not sin*—viz., he was God—and why it is that he *did not sin*—viz., he was the human Jesus, anointed and empowered by the Spirit—in fact presents us with an answer to this theological problem that promises to account fully for the genuineness of both his impeccability and his temptations. Having given a summary of this proposal, allow me to develop it just a bit.

First, we begin by affirming what is in some ways both the clear-

[17] I appreciate much Gerald F. Hawthorne's profound study *The Presence and the Power: The Significance of the Holy Spirit in the Life and Ministry of Jesus* (Dallas: Word, 1991). More recently, John E. McKinley has produced a work of major significance on this issue, arguing in ways that are similar to the proposal I here describe briefly. See his *Tempted for Us: Theological Models and the Practical Relevance of Christ's Impeccability and Temptation* (Carlisle, Cumbria, UK: Paternoster, 2009). And for an insightful study of Christ's temptations and how they relate to the Christian life, see Russell D. Moore, *Tempted and Tried: Temptation and the Triumph of Christ* (Wheaton, IL: Crossway, 2011).

est and most important truth in the whole of this discussion, viz., that Christ in fact did not sin. Scripture here is abundantly clear: "[God] made [Christ] to be sin who knew no sin, so that in him we might become the righteousness of God" (2 Cor. 5:21); "[Christ] in every respect has been tempted as we are, yet without sin" (Heb. 4:15); "You have been called for this purpose, since Christ also suffered for you, leaving you an example that you should follow in His steps, who committed no sin, nor was any deceit found in His mouth" (1 Pet. 2:21–22 NASB) with a quotation here from Isa. 53:9); and "You know that He appeared in order to take away sins, and in Him there is no sin" (1 John 3:5 NASB).

Second, the impeccability of Christ is a reasonable inference from Scripture's teaching about who the incarnate Christ is, and an inference so clear and compelling that it is unreasonable to imagine Jesus not considering this inference, thereby knowing the truth of his own impeccability. I agree here with Shedd, who argued that if Christ could sin, "the guilt would not be confined to the human nature" but the divine nature also would be stained.[18] Since this cannot occur to the immutably holy divine nature, once the union of human and divine natures has occurred, the human nature is rendered impeccable by virtue of its union to the impeccable divine nature.

Or one might think of the issue in these terms: since the Holy One born of Mary was fully God as well as fully man, this seems to imply some limitations in expression both for his divine and human natures. That is, not only would the union of natures require some limitation in the expression of certain divine attributes in order for him to live an authentic human life—e.g., Christ both grew in wisdom and had limited knowledge (e.g., Luke 2:40, 52)—but also some limitation of his human choice and activity would likewise be entailed, so that no action that might threaten the integrity or holiness of his divine nature could occur.

Now, this is not to say that Christ did not have experiences that were distinctive and unique to his deity or humanity, respectively.

---

[18] Shedd, *Dogmatic Theology*, 334.

Rather, it is to say that no expression of either his deity or his humanity could violate the integrity of the other nature. So, for example, Jesus can forgive sin as God (e.g., Mark 2:5ff), yet this action does not violate the integrity of his human nature although it surely does extend beyond the abilities and limitations of that human nature. Similarly, Jesus can become hungry (e.g., Luke 4:2) or thirsty (e.g., John 19:28), yet these genuinely human experiences do not violate Jesus's divine nature, since nothing in that divine nature corresponds to the experience of physical hunger or thirst.

But one cannot say the same thing about the hypothetical possibility of the theanthropic Jesus sinning. Even Erickson, who wants to say that Jesus could have sinned, is unwilling to say that Jesus *qua* theanthropic person—i.e., as the person comprised of human and divine natures in union—could have sinned. Why? Erickson, Shedd, Bavinck, and nearly all have understood that if the theanthropic Jesus sinned, the moral substance of this action could not be divorced from his divine nature. Unlike Jesus's experiences of hunger or thirst, which correspond to nothing comparable in his divine nature, if the theanthropic Jesus sinned, this moral act—or more precisely, this immoral act—does correspond to something in the divine nature, namely, God's own holy, moral nature. Hence, unless one imagines the break of natures that Erickson proposes, the theanthropic Jesus, as God and man united indissolubly in one person, could not sin.[19]

Third, and most important for the position I am here arguing, the impeccability of Christ by virtue of his impeccable divine nature united to his human nature has nothing directly to do with how he resisted temptation and how it was that he did not sin. Yes, Christ was impeccable, but his impeccability is quite literally irrelevant to explaining his sinlessness. The common evangelical intuition seems to be this: if the reason Christ *could* not sin is that he is God, then the reason Christ *did* not sin must likewise be that he is God. My

---

[19] See the helpful critique of Erickson's proposed hypothetical breaking of the union of the human and divine natures in Jesus, were his sinning to be envisioned, in Garrett J. DeWeese, "One Person, Two Natures: Two Metaphysical Models of the Incarnation," in Issler and Sanders, *Jesus in Trinitarian Perspective*, 128–30.

proposal denies this symmetry and insists that the questions of why Christ *could not sin* and why he *did not sin* require, instead, remarkably different answers.

To understand better the distinction here invoked between why something *could not* occur and why it *did not* occur, consider with me two illustrations. First, imagine a swimmer who wants to attempt breaking the world's record for the longest continuous swim (which, I've read, is something over 70 miles). As this swimmer trains, besides his daily swims of 5 to 10 miles he includes weekly swims of greater distance. On some of the longer swims of 30 and 40 miles, he notices that his muscles can begin to tighten and cramp a bit, and he becomes worried that in attempting to break the world record, his muscles may cramp severely and he could then drown. So, he consults with friends, and they decide to arrange for a boat to follow along behind the swimmer 20 or 30 feet back, close enough to pick him up should any serious problem arise but far enough away so as not to interfere with the attempted historic swim itself. On the appointed day, conditions being just right, the swimmer dives in and begins his attempt at breaking the world record. As he swims, the boat follows along comfortably behind, ready to pick him up if needed. But no help is needed; with determination and resolve, the swimmer relentlessly swims and swims and swims, and in due time he succeeds in breaking the world record.

Now, consider two questions: (1) Why is it that in this record-breaking event the swimmer *could not have drowned*? The answer is that the boat was there all the while, ready to rescue him if needed. But (2) Why is it the swimmer *did not drown*? The answer is that he kept swimming! Notice that the answer to the second question has nothing at all to do with the boat, i.e., it has nothing to do with the answer to the first question. In fact, if you gave the answer of "the boat" to question 2, the swimmer would be both astonished and dismayed. It simply is not true that the swimmer did not drown because the boat was there. The boat, quite literally, had absolutely nothing to do with why the swimmer did not drown. Furthermore, although the swimmer knew full well that he could not drown due to the boat's following along behind him, that knowledge had nothing to do with why he did not drown, since he also knew that if he ever relied on the boat, his mission of breaking the world record would be forfeited. So although he knew that he could not drown due to the boat, he also knew that he could only accomplish his goal by swimming as if there were no boat there at all.

Second, imagine a high school student who excels in math. A major exam is coming, one for which the teacher has allowed students to use calculators. But this student chooses to keep his calculator in his pocket throughout the exam. He knows that if he uses his calculator, the exam (for him!) would be a breeze, and he would get a perfect score with no problem whatsoever. But instead, he does all the equations and problem solving in long-hand on paper and simply out of his head. He is committed to working his hardest to ace this exam without using the calculator he has with him. When exams are returned, our student is the only one to receive 100 percent. When a friend from another class hears of his perfect score, he says to our student, "Well, of course you got a perfect score on the exam, because I heard that your teacher allowed all of you to use your calculators." "Ah," our student replies, "yes, I *could* have used my calculator, but I *did* the exam instead completely on my own without making use of it at all." So, why is it that our gifted student, in taking this exam, *could not* have failed to get a perfect score? He could have used his calculator, assuring him that he'd get 100 percent. But why is it that our gifted student *did not* fail to get a perfect score on the exam? He used his head and worked hard. The presence of the calculator was irrelevant to our student's achieving his perfect score. Perhaps these illustrations are sufficient to help convey both the legitimacy and the importance of this distinction between why something *could not* happen and why it *did not* happen. Although Christ was fully God, and as fully God he could not sin, he deliberately did not appeal, as it were, to his divine nature in fighting the temptations that came to him. As a human, he not only could be tempted but was tempted in the greatest ways any human has been tempted in all of history. Yet for every temptation he faced, he fought and resisted fully and totally apart from any use of or appeal to his intrinsic divine nature.

As one considers again the temptations of Christ, it seems that one should rightly hold that the theanthropic Jesus *could not sin* because he was God. But this does not necessarily answer the question of why he *did not sin*. And, in fact, the answer Scripture suggests to us is this: Jesus did not sin, not because he relied on the supernatural power of his divine nature or because his divine nature overpowered his human nature, keeping him from sinning, but because he utilized all of the resources given to him in his humanity. He loved and meditated on God's Word (consider again the significance here of Psalm 1 being the first and opening psalm, pointing obviously to Christ); he prayed to his Father; he trusted in the wisdom and rightness of his Father's will and Word; and, very significantly, he relied on the supernatural power of the Spirit to strengthen him to do all that he was called upon to do. Jesus lived his life in reliance on the Spirit so that his resistance to temptation and his obedience to the will of the Father took place through, not apart from, the empowerment provided him as the second Adam, the seed of Abraham, the son of David. Recall again Peter's claim that God anointed Jesus "with the Holy Spirit and with power," and that he went about doing good (the moral life and obedience of Christ) as well as healing all who are oppressed by the Devil (the miracles he performed), "for God was with him" (Acts 10:38). Although he was God, and although he was impeccable as the God-man, he resisted temptation and obeyed the Father not by his divine nature but by the power of the Spirit who indwelt him.

Furthermore, could Christ have known that as the theanthropic Savior he was genuinely impeccable yet still be genuinely tempted? Clearly the answer is yes, since he also knew that his mission was to obey where Adam failed, to live his life as the perfectly obedient man, through the power of the Spirit. He knew that to rely on his divine nature would be to forfeit the mission on which he was sent. Just as our swimmer could only achieve his record-breaking victory without ever making use of the boat that was there to assure his safety, and as our math student could only earn a perfect exam score on his own by keeping his calculator in his pocket, so Jesus knew his mission required that he fight temptation—every temptation, every time!—by making use solely of those resources that were provided him in his humanity. And so he did. For our sake and for our salvation, he steeled his heart to fight temptation as a man, in dependence on his Father and by the power of the Spirit. Praise be to Jesus who, though tempted in every way as we are, never, ever sinned.

THE EXTENT AND FORCE OF CHRIST'S TEMPTATIONS

One more question should be addressed in light of what we have just seen. We've argued that the temptations of Christ were real and genuine and that, although he was fully God, he fought those temptations as a man, filled with the Spirit. Thus Jesus could be and was genuinely impeccable while also being genuinely tempted. Given the genuineness of the temptations of Christ, we wish now to ask this: Just how extensive were those temptations, and how great was the difficulty our Savior faced in resisting them in order to be the sinless Savior that he had to be to bring about our salvation?

There are two elements to our answer. First, it stands to reason that Jesus was faced with the most difficult and relentless barrage of temptations that anyone ever has received. After all, Satan knew what was at stake in Jesus's coming. Satan's offer to Christ of the kingdoms of the world (Luke 4:5–8) indicates his knowledge of just why Christ had come. He knew that Christ's work would destroy everything he had built, that the establishing of Christ's kingdom would bring an end to his dominion, and so he brought upon Christ the most difficult temptations he could possibly conceive. Furthermore, Satan knew how many sins it would take to make Jesus a sinner. The answer here is astonishing, when you think of the full life that Jesus lived. One sin, and one only, would do the trick. Satan needed to trip up Jesus *only once* to bring an end to this threat against the kingdom of darkness over which he reigned. So the force and relentless nature of Satan's temptations against Christ surely surpassed anything Satan has ever done to anyone else.

I think this point is helpful when the suggestion is made that our temptations must be greater than Christ's were, since we have sinful natures and he didn't. And it is true—Christ was not born with the sin of Adam (he was the second Adam), and because he never sinned, his human nature was not stained with sin. Our natures are deeply sinful, to be sure, so some have thought that the temptations that arise out of our sinful cravings must surpass in difficulty the temptations Christ had. But this suggestion fails to take into account the heightened force that Satan would have brought against Jesus. Granted, Christ was not tempted through a sinful nature, as we are. But Christ was faced with the strongest and most relentless barrage of temptations Satan has devised for anyone. I think we can justifiably assume that what he lacked in terms of internal temptations from a sinful nature, he experienced in far greater measure from the external temptations Satan directly, forcefully, and relentlessly brought against him.

Second, because Jesus never sinned, he fought every temptation, every time, fully, experiencing the unmitigated force of each temptation until he had succeeded in defeating each one, coming out the other side victorious. Isn't it clear to any of us who think about the sin of our own lives that one of the reasons we give into temptation is that the pressure is off and the battle is ended once we have given in? The immediate sense of release from the struggle is deeply appealing when we don't want to keep fighting! So, marvel at our *sinless* Savior. Because he never sinned when tempted, this means that he fought every temptation fully to the end. He never, not once, gave into that delicious and enticing longing simply to end the struggle by yielding to the temptation. Rather, he fought and fought and fought, in every temptation, every time, always coming out the other side victorious. Surely his struggle in the garden of Gethsemane illustrates just this. Why did Jesus pray three times, even sweating drops of blood in his agony, over obeying the will of his Father? Was it not because he had to keep fighting in order to win? His obedience here was extremely difficult, and the fight had to be engaged. As the temptation continued, so the battle also had to continue. So, marvel at this: our Savior fought every temptation, every time, all the way to the end, and never once gave in. Marvel and wonder and worship.

APPLICATION

1) What a difference it makes to know that Jesus lived his life as one of us, fighting temptation with resources given to him in his human nature. We see in this that victory over temptation really can happen! The resources God gives—particularly his Word, prayer, and the power of the Spirit—are there for us as they were there for Jesus. We can look at Jesus with a realization that he lived the kind of life we too are called to live, and he made use of the very means that are given also to us. Such hope and confidence is grounded in this understanding of Jesus's resisting temptation fully as a human. We look to Jesus and we have hope. Human life lived in obedience to the Father has been done by him, and we have every reason to trust in God's grace to see our obedience increase as we make use of what God makes available to us, as he did for Jesus.

2) Of course, whether we make use of the resources becomes one of the key questions in our sanctification and resistance of temptation. Having a mind saturated with the Word of God, as Jesus had, doesn't just happen. Having a life of fervent and regular prayer, as Jesus had, won't magically appear. Learning to trust the power of the Spirit when tempted, as Jesus did, isn't automatic. When will we learn that although the Christian life is lived by grace, the grace of God at work within us seeks to activate us, not replace us, in taking up the activities of spiritual living necessary for us to grow as we should? We may sing, "May the mind of Christ my Savior, live in me from day to day," but if we don't read diligently and meditate regularly on the Word of Christ, we simply will not have the mind of Christ. So while we can rightly look to Jesus with hope, seeing in him a true human who has faced and won the battle with temptation, we also must see in him a man who gave himself, with diligence and longing, to a life devoted to the Word of God, to prayer, and to reliance on the Spirit. In our longing to share in his victory over temptation, let us also share in his devotion to all that is needed to strengthen our minds and hearts and souls.

3) Rejoice that though Christ was tempted in every way as we are, he never sinned! Since his obedience was not automatic, since he fought fervently every time to the full extent necessary to defeat each temptation brought to him, we should give to him our deepest expressions of thanks and praise. How amazing that he never sinned! How remarkable was his perfect obedience! And since nothing less was required of the one who would take our place and die for our sins, we stand amazed at this human Jesus, who succeeded every day of his life in living in obedience to his Father. What a man! What an example! What a Savior!

DISCUSSION QUESTIONS

1) Hebrews 4:15 tells us that Jesus "in every respect has been tempted as we are, yet without sin." As you reflect on this verse, what is the impact in your own life as you consider that Jesus was tempted "in every respect" as you are, and that he endured each of these temptations "without sin"?

2) How important is it to know that these are *real* temptations, and that Jesus's successful resistance of these temptations was not automatic but rather was hard fought and hard won? How does your understanding of Jesus differ if you think that he resisted temptation from his divine nature as opposed to his human nature?

3) Consider the resources that God gave to Jesus to use in his fight against temptation. Most principally, he was given the Word of God, prayer, the community of faith, and the gift of the supernatural Holy Spirit. Think through the life of Christ and reflect on how he made use of these various resources. How did he use each one? What effect did each have on his ability to resist temptation and obey the Father?

4) We are called to follow in Jesus's steps, which means we should make use of the same resources that he did. Reflect for a moment on each of these resources. How well are you using the resource of the Word of God? Of prayer? Of fellow believers and their support? Of reliance on the Holy Spirit?

5) If we are serious about defeating temptation in our lives, and if we are serious about growing in our obedience before God, we must consider seriously how we can make better use of the enabling gifts God grants us for our growth, our sanctification, and our obedience. So a good question to ask is this: how can we grow in making better use of these divine gifts to empower us to resist temptation and obey our Lord Christ? What are some specific ways we can see growth in understanding and utilizing these gifts?

6

LIVING AS A MAN

Therefore he had to be made like his brothers in every respect, so that he might become a merciful and faithful high priest in the service of God, to make propitiation for the sins of the people.

HEBREWS 2:17

1) Jesus Christ of Nazareth was fully God. (2) Jesus Christ of Nazareth was fully human. (3) Jesus Christ of Nazareth was a male human being.

All three of those statements are judged to be true in the orthodox tradition, and each is borne out by abundant biblical testimony. The first two are often stated together as necessarily true for the occurrence of the incarnation and substitutionary atonement. Anselm's classic treatment, *Cur Deus Homo*, spells out why an atoning sacrifice required that Jesus be both divine and human: divine, to be of sufficient value to pay fully and finally for the sin of the world and satisfy the offence against the honor of God; human, to die as a fit substitute in our place. But, the question of whether Jesus had to be a *male* human being has seldom been discussed until recently. Was his male gender merely an arbitrary feature of the incarnational design? Did the Father throw dice or draw straws in choosing to send the Messiah as a male human being? Or was the male gender of Jesus essential to the reality of his incarnational identity and to the accomplishment of his incarnational mission? In other words, did Jesus have to be male, or could our Savior have been a woman?

A couple of recent developments raise this question to a level of higher poignancy. I have in mind, first, the publication in 1995 of *The*

New Testament and Psalms: An Inclusive Version,[1] in which it was decided that the male gender of Jesus had no "christological significance, or significance for salvation."[2] As the editors explain,

> When in the Gospels the historical person, Jesus, is referred to as "son," the word is retained. But when Jesus is called "Son of God" or "Son of the Blessed One," and the maleness of the historical person Jesus is not relevant, but the "Son's" intimate relation to the "Father" is being spoken about (see Mt 11.25–27), the formal equivalent "Child" is used for "Son," and gender-specific pronouns referring to the "Child" are avoided. Thus readers are enabled to identify themselves with Jesus' *humanity*.
>
> If the fact that Jesus was a man, and not a woman, has no christological significance in the New Testament, then neither does the fact that Jesus was a *son* and not a *daughter*. If Jesus is identified as "Son," believers of both sexes become "sons" of God, but if Jesus is called "Child," believers of both sexes can understand themselves as "children of God."[3]

And a few pages later, they assert:

> A "son" is a male offspring, and the historical person Jesus was, of course, a man. But that Jesus was a male person was not thought in the early church to have christological significance, or significance for salvation. It was not Jesus' maleness that was believed to save males, but Jesus' humanness that was believed to save human beings. As was said by many theologians in the early church, what was not assumed (by Jesus) was not saved. . . .
>
> If the fact that Jesus was a "son" and not a "daughter" has no theological significance, then we are justified in rendering the Greek *huios* (usually "son") as "Child" or "Child of God" instead of "Son" when it occurs in a christological sense. In this version gender-specific pronouns are not used when referring to the "Child," thus enabling all readers to identify themselves with Jesus' *humanity*. When Jesus is identified as "Son," believers, as heirs, become "sons"; but when Jesus is identified as "Child," believers become "children of God"—both women and men.[4]

---

[1] Victor R. Gold et al., eds., *The New Testament and Psalms: An Inclusive Version* (New York: Oxford University Press, 1995).
[2] Ibid., *xvii.*
[3] Ibid., *xiii* (emphasis original).
[4] Ibid., *xvii–xviii* (emphasis original).

A second reason for raising the question of whether our Savior could have been a woman is the rendering of Jesus's gender in certain passages, first in the *Today's New International Version* (hereafter TNIV) released in 2002 from the International Bible Society and Zondervan, and now more recently in the 2011 New International Version (hereafter NIV 2011). For example, consider Hebrews 2:17 in the NIV (1984), TNIV, and NIV 2011, respectively:

> NIV: For this reason he had to be made like his *brothers* in every way, in order that he might become a merciful and faithful high priest in service to God, and that he might make atonement for the sins of the people.

> TNIV: For this reason he had to be made like his *brothers and sisters* in every way, in order that he might become a merciful and faithful high priest in service to God, and that he might make atonement for the sins of the people.

> NIV 2011: For this reason he had to be made like *them, fully human in every way*, in order that he might become a merciful and faithful high priest in service to God, and that he might make atonement for the sins of the people.

For the TNIV to turn "brothers" into "brothers and sisters" leads inevitably to confusion and possible misunderstanding.[5] What was Jesus's gender, anyway? one wonders. Just how was he somehow like his "sisters in every way"? To speak specifically of the gender of "sisters" and say that Christ was "like" them "in every way" at least leads one to wonder whether the male gender of Jesus was at all significant in the incarnation and atonement. Although Jesus was a man (we know from other texts), from this passage we might be prompted to ask, might our Savior just as well have been a woman? Evidently this very problem was also seen by the translators, so the NIV 2011 has

---

[5] I agree with Wayne Grudem's comment on this text: "Did Jesus have to become like his sisters 'in every way' in order to become a 'high priest in service to God'? All the Old Testament priests were men, and surely the high priest was a man. This text does not quite proclaim an androgynous Jesus (who was both male and female), but it surely leaves open a wide door for misunderstanding, and almost invites misunderstanding." "A Brief Summary of Concerns About the TNIV," *Journal for Biblical Manhood and Womanhood*, 7.2 (Fall 2002): 7.

made a significant change, and this for the better, to be sure. They recognize the need to stress the common humanity of Christ, which of course is implied in the NIV rendering, obscured in the TNIV, but now made clear in the NIV 2011.

Or consider 1 Corinthians 15:21–22:

> NIV: For since death came through a *man*, the resurrection of the dead comes also through a *man*. For as in Adam all die, so in Christ all will be made alive.

> TNIV: For since death came through a *human being*, the resurrection of the dead comes also through a *human being*. For as in Adam all die, so in Christ all will be made alive.

> NIV 2011: For since death came through a *man*, the resurrection of the dead comes also through a *man*. For as in Adam all die, so in Christ all will be made alive.

Clearly what the TNIV has said here is true. But the change from "man" to "human being" does lead one to wonder whether there is any significance to the male gender of either Adam or of Christ. Could Adam, *qua* head of the race, have been a woman? This seems like an odd question, does it not, since Adam had a wife, who clearly might instead have been seen as the head of the human race? After all, she sinned first! But, since it was Adam, not the woman, whom Paul points to here, and since Adam was male, is it best to eliminate the male term in reference to him? And so of Christ. Is it best to drop out of view the male gender of Christ, the second Adam? Again, a reader of the TNIV might wonder, from this verse, whether it matters that Jesus came as a male Messiah. Could our Savior have been, instead, a woman? But now in the NIV 2011 the translators have reverted to the NIV reading. Evidently they, too, saw the obviousness of the "maleness" of both Adam and Christ and so returned to this more natural reading.

Consider one more reference, 1 Timothy 2:5:

> NIV: For there is one God and one mediator between God and *men*, the *man* Christ Jesus.

TNIV: For there is one God and one mediator between God and *human beings*, Christ Jesus, *himself human.*

NIV 2011: For there is one God and one mediator between God and *mankind*, the *man* Christ Jesus.

The change from the NIV to the TNIV is significant. Instead of indicating that Christ, the mediator, is a man, who would obviously also be understood as human—as in the NIV and again in the NIV 2011— here Christ is generically and explicitly human, whose human nature comes in the form of a male human, as implied by the insertion of "himself" (TNIV). Again, though, we wonder whether it is merely accidental (in the Aristotelian sense, as nonessential) and not necessary that Christ was in fact a male human being. If it is the "human" identity of Jesus alone that matters in his being our mediator, then might the question arise, could our Savior have been a woman?

What significance is attached to the historical fact that the incarnate Son of God, the eternal Word who took on human flesh, came into this world as a man (i.e., as a male human being)? Does Scripture give us reason to think that his male gender does or does not have theological and soteriological importance? Is it necessary that the Savior be born, live, and die as a man, or could our Savior have been a woman?

THEOLOGICAL NECESSITY OF THE MALE GENDER OF OUR SAVIOR

Consider with me a number of reasons (twelve, to be exact) for concluding that the male gender of Jesus was essential both to the reality of his incarnational identity and to the accomplishment of his incarnational mission.

1) First and most basic, Jesus Christ's preincarnate existence and identity is clearly revealed to be that of the *eternal Son* of the Father. As Jesus says in John 6:37–38, "All that the Father gives me will come to me, and whoever comes to me I will never cast out. I have *come down from heaven*, not to do my own will but the will of him who

sent me," i.e., the will of his Father in heaven. And in John 6:44 Jesus continues, "No one can come to me unless the *Father who sent me* draws him." Clearly, Jesus understands that he has come down from heaven, that he has been sent to earth to fulfill the mission for which he was sent, and that it is the Father (in heaven) who sent the Son (from heaven to earth) to do this work (see John 3:17; Gal. 4:4; Heb. 1:1–2). As Augustine has put this point,

> For the Son is from the Father, not the Father from the Son. In the light of this we can now perceive that the Son is not just said to have been sent because the Word became flesh, but that *he was sent in order for the Word to become flesh*, and by this bodily presence to do all that was written. That is, we should understand that it was not just the man who the Word became that was sent, but that *the Word was sent to become man*. For he was not sent in virtue of some disparity of power or substance or anything in him that was not equal to the Father, but in virtue of the Son being from the Father, not the Father being from the Son.[6]

The Son, then, is the eternal Son of the Father; and the Father is the eternal Father of the Son. This relationship stands apart from the created order and the incarnation itself, while it is also true that this relationship accounts, in part, for the created order (i.e., the Father creates through the Son, e.g., Col. 1:12–16) and the incarnation (i.e., the Word of John's prologue displays the "glory of the Father," e.g., John 1:14).

Now, as it is true that God is not in essence male, so also is it true that neither the eternal Father nor the eternal Son is male; neither the divine essence, nor the eternal persons of the Godhead are gendered, literally and really. So why is the first person of the Trinity the eternal "Father," and the second person the eternal "Son"? Must this not be the language God has chosen to indicate the type of eternal relationship that exists between the first and second persons? If the "Son" is sent by the "Father," and if the "Son" comes to do the will of the "Father," does it not stand to reason that God wishes by this lan-

---

[6] St. Augustine, *The Trinity*, trans. Edmund Hill, vol. 5 of *The Works of St. Augustine* (Brooklyn, NY: New City Press, 1991) 4.27 (emphasis added).

guage to indicate something of the authority and submission that exist within the relationships of the members of the immanent Trinity? Furthermore, while that point alone (i.e., of authority and submission) might have been communicated with "Mother" and "Daughter," the choice for "Father" and "Son" also indicates something of the Father's role over all of creation, and the Son's role in creation and, more particularly, in the incarnational mission. The first person of the Godhead chooses to name himself "Father" (not "Mother") to indicate the respect and honor that is due him, as he anticipates in the created order the role that he will give to earthly fathers as the leaders or the heads of their homes (e.g., Mal. 1:6; cf. Jer. 49:13, 18; Ezek. 35:9; Obad. 10). Likewise, he gives to the second person, who stands under his authority, the name of "Son," both as the appropriate name in relation to him as eternal Father but also as most appropriate in depicting the Son who will come to save and then be the groom-head over his bride, the church (e.g., Eph. 5:22–33; Rev. 19:7; 21:2, 9). That Christ in his preincarnate state is the eternal Son of the eternal Father stands as strong theological basis for believing that the incarnate one, viz., the human nature that is joined with the divine nature of the second person of the Trinity, must then himself be a male human being. The eternal Son must be joined with a human son (*not* daughter), so that the incarnate Christ may express to the world both his relation to the Father, i.e., as the Son of the Father, and his relation to the church, i.e., as the Savior, Lord, head, and groom of the church.

Now, some might wonder this: Could it be that the second person of the Trinity came as a man only because of a patriarchal culture into which he descended in first-century Israel? Had the second person come to a matriarchal culture, might "she" come as a woman? Two brief comments are in order. (1) Is it reasonable to look at the way God made man and woman respectively, and conclude from this that women might just as well have been the power brokers throughout the cultures of the world? Clearly, God made men stronger and bigger, as a gender, and he made women able to give birth to, feed, and nurture children. By these fundamental God-designed differences, shall we think that God considered that the dominant "power" of the sexes might have gone the other way? (2) The second person of the Trinity was eternally under the authority of the first person, and this is true regardless of what you call them. Authority and submission inhere in the Trinity itself, and this same authority and submission relationship is reflected in the created order. So if God chooses to invest in males a kind of headship (i.e., authority) in the community of faith and in the home, then God will declare his identity to us in ways fitting that design. He will choose masculine terminology as his self-descriptors, because a fundamental patriarchalism (i.e., male headship) was by his own design. What we must watch out for is a progression (digression) from rejecting male headship as part of the created design of God for the human race, to the natural extension of then questioning the legitimacy of masculine God-language generally, and then to questioning the necessity of the male identity of the Messiah particularly.

2) Our Savior must have been a man since he came as the second Adam, the man who stands as head over his new and redeemed race. It is remarkable that although the woman sinned first in the garden (Gen. 3:6), God went first to the man (Gen. 3:9), and clearly he holds the man primarily responsible for the sin of the human race (Rom. 5:12–19; 1 Cor. 15:21–22). Notice particularly in Romans 5:12–21 the emphasis on "*one* man's trespass" (v. 15), "*one* man's sin" and "*one* trespass" (v. 16), "*one* man's trespass" and "*one* man" (v. 17), "*one* trespass" (v. 18), and "*one* man's disobedience" (v. 19). The woman is conspicuously absent from the discussion. Although she sinned first, God created man as the responsible leader in this relationship (cf. 1 Cor. 11:7–9; 1 Tim. 2:13–15), and God holds him morally culpable for the sin, by his "one" act of disobedience, that spreads to the whole human race (Rom. 5:12).

So the logic of 1 Corinthians 15:21–22 is clear. As Adam was head over his race, bringing it bondage and death, so now Christ is head over his race, bringing it liberation and resurrection life. In light of the background of the sin in the garden, where God holds the first Adam (*qua* male) in particular responsible for sin, it is clear now that Christ the second Adam (yes, *male* human being, as Adam was the male human of the pair in the garden) brings reclamation and restoration to what the first Adam had destroyed. So it is that by a *man* came death and by a *man* has come also the resurrection of the dead. Yes, both first and second Adams are *human*. But also essential to a proper biblical understanding is that both are *male* humans, not female.

3) The Abrahamic covenant requires that the Savior to come as the promised descendant of Abraham would be a man. Admittedly, it is not clear from the original covenant, given to Abraham in Genesis 12, that the fulfillment would come through Abraham's male, and not female, offspring. No gender specificity is indicated; rather, all we read is that God would make of Abraham a great nation and that through him all the families of the earth would be blessed (Gen. 12:2–3). Likewise, the repetition of the covenant in Genesis 15 lacks gender specificity,[7] continuing the same language of Genesis 12 of "offspring" who will come from Abraham numbering as many as the stars (Gen. 15:3–5). Granted, one might conjecture that the promise to Abraham would be fulfilled through a son, not a daughter, since God has already established a pattern of highlighting the male line (e.g., Adam, Noah, now Abraham), and since Abraham himself proposed Eliezer of Damascus (a male) as the promised heir. Nonetheless, no specific gender reference is yet given.

The repetition of the covenant in Genesis 17, however, makes clear that it is a son, and a son born to Abraham and Sarah in their old age, who will be the promised heir, the one through whom God's covenant pledge will begin to be fulfilled. That Sarah (not Hagar) would be the mother of the son of promise, God specifies in Genesis 17:16: "I will bless her [Sarah], and moreover, I will give you a son by her. I will bless her, and she shall become nations; kings of peoples shall come from her." Sarah was the chosen instrument through whom the son of promise would come, and through her son, kings (male leaders of nations) would then arise. When Abraham protests God's stated plan, owing to Sarah's advanced age, and so pleads with God to accept Ishmael, God again repeats the promise and plan: "God said, 'No, but Sarah your wife shall bear you a son, and you shall call his name Isaac.

---

[7] The ESV translation of Gen. 15:4, "Your very own son shall be your heir," anticipates the promise to Abraham from Genesis 17, for Gen. 15:4 literally is, "one from your own loins."

I will establish my covenant with him as an everlasting covenant for his offspring after him'" (v. 19).

As the genealogies of Jesus Christ in Matthew 1 and Luke 3 indicate, the Abrahamic covenant was fulfilled through the succession of sons born from Abraham down to Jesus himself. And surely Paul echoes this same understanding in Galatians 3 when he speaks of the "offspring," not "offsprings" of Abraham, who is none other than Christ (v. 16). As Paul summarizes this point, "in Christ Jesus the blessing of Abraham might come to the Gentiles, so that we might receive the promised Spirit through faith" (v. 14). And so it is clear that both in the giving of the Abrahamic covenant and in its fulfillment in Christ, it is essential that the one who comes as the ultimate promised heir (the singular "offspring," as Paul indicates) would be born in the line of Abraham, and this one must be a "son" of Abraham, i.e., a male offspring.

4) The Davidic covenant explicitly requires that the one who will reign forever on the throne of David be a son of David. God's promise to David recorded in 2 Samuel 7:12–13 reads: "When your days are fulfilled and you lie down with your fathers, I will raise up your offspring after you, who shall come from your body, and I will establish his kingdom. He shall build a house for my name, and I will establish the throne of his kingdom forever." Here there is no ambiguity; the promised heir of the throne of David, who will one day reign forever, will be a son of David, i.e., a male descendant who will be king on David's throne.

Both Ezekiel 34:23–24 and 37:24–28 indicate the ongoing longing and expectation that "David" (i.e., a son of David fulfilling the Davidic covenant) will come as Israel's king and reign over a land of peace and righteousness. And again here, as with the Abrahamic covenant, the genealogies of Matthew 1 and Luke 3 indicate a line of sons leading from David down to the birth of Jesus Christ. The angel Gabriel made clear to Mary that her son, Jesus, would be this long-awaited "David," establishing his throne forever, for he tells Mary, "And behold, you will conceive in your womb and bear a son, and you shall call his name Jesus. He will be great and will be called the Son of the Most High. And the Lord God will give to him the throne of his father David, and he will reign over the house of Jacob forever, and of his kingdom there will be no end" (Luke 1:31–33). Clearly here also, then, we see that the Savior to come, the long-awaited son of David, must be a male offspring from David himself.

5) The new covenant of Jeremiah 31:31–34 requires that the Savior will actually accomplish the forgiveness of sins it promises, and to do this, the Savior must be male. Jeremiah 31:34 gives, as the basis of its promise of a new covenant with the house of Israel and house of Judah, this pledge: "For I will forgive their iniquity, and I will remember their sin no more." But one must inquire how Israel's sin will be removed forever and for all of God's people. Anticipating the argument from Hebrews, that the sacrifice of bulls and goats cannot actually and efficaciously take away sin, how then would God lead his people to think that this forgiveness, in such full and final way, can occur? Surely, the answer is found in the Suffering Servant whom Isaiah presents, who would bear our griefs and sorrows and have laid on him the iniquity of us all (Isa. 53:4–6). But clearly, this one who "makes an offering for guilt" (v. 10) and bears "the sin of many" (v. 12) is none other than the "man of sorrows" who is despised and rejected by others (v. 3). The one who will provide the basis for the realization of new-covenant forgiveness is this man.

Luke's account of the Last Supper of Jesus with his disciples confirms this understanding. Here, Jesus, the man of sorrows (the anguish of Gethsemane was just hours away), took the cup and handed it to his disciples, saying, "This cup is the new covenant in my blood" (Luke 22:21; cf. 1 Cor. 11:25). And so we see that this man Jesus, by his broken body and shed blood, is the one through whom the new covenant is inaugurated and its promised forgiveness realized. Our Savior, then, must be this man of sorrows.

6) The Savior must come as a prophet like unto Moses, as predicted by Moses and fulfilled in Jesus Christ. In Deuteronomy 18:15, Moses declares, "The LORD your God will raise up for you a prophet like me from among you, from your brothers—it is to him you shall listen." Clearly, then, this one who comes as a prophet like Moses

must be male. Even though some of Israel's prophetic voices were female, most were male; yet this prophet, the one like unto Moses, must be a man.

The apostle Peter understands this promise from the Lord through Moses to be fulfilled in Jesus Christ. Speaking in Solomon's Portico shortly after the healing of a lame beggar, Peter accounts for this miracle by appeal to the power of Christ, experienced by faith in him. And Christ, says Peter, is the one spoken of by the mouth of the holy prophets, for "Moses said, 'The Lord God will raise up for you a prophet like me from your brothers. You shall listen to him in whatever he tells you'" (Acts 3:22). The prophet like unto Moses, then, promised by Moses himself and fulfilled in Christ, must have been a man.

7) Our new and permanent High Priest, whose office is secured as sins are atoned for and full pardon is pleaded on our behalf before the Father, must be a man. While there were some prophetesses (i.e., female prophets) in Israel, there simply were no female priests. Aaron and his sons, not daughters, were the priests of Israel. So one would expect that the final and permanent High Priest, who makes atonement once for all, would be a man. And so it is.

The High Priest, Jesus, however, comes not in the Aaronic or Levitical line of priests but in the order of Melchizedek, explains Hebrews. And, as Hebrews 7 ends its argument, it is made explicit that this priest is the Son spoken of in Hebrews 1. Concerning Christ we read: "He has no need, like those high priests, to offer sacrifices daily, first for his own sins and then for those of the people, since he did this once for all when he offered up himself. For the law appoints men in their weakness as high priests, but the word of the oath, which came later than the law, appoints a Son who has been made perfect forever" (Heb. 7:27–28). The Son, then, is our eternal High Priest, who pleads his own offering for sin done once for all. Our Savior as High and Eternal Priest, must have been a man.

8) Not only did our Savior come as the last and greatest prophet, like unto Moses, and as the High and Eternal Priest, but he also came as the glorious King of kings, reigning over the nations in splendor

and righteousness. But if our Savior is to be king, he must come as a man.

Isaiah 9:6–7 records familiar words about the prophesied coming of this King, "For unto us a child is born, to us a son is given, and the government shall be upon his shoulder, and his name shall be called Wonderful Counselor, Mighty God, Everlasting Father, Prince of Peace. Of the increase of his government and of peace there will be no end, on the throne of David and over his kingdom, to establish it and to uphold it with justice and with righteousness from this time forth and forevermore. The zeal of the LORD of hosts will do this." From this text alone it is clear that this king will be male. He is the "son" given, and he is called "Everlasting Father" and "Prince of Peace." He sits on the "throne of David" where he reigns forevermore.

Consider also Hebrews' use of Psalm 45:6–7 in announcing Christ's reign as king: "Your throne, O God, is forever and ever, the scepter of your kingdom is a scepter of uprightness." Clearly, this King, as God's Son, is male. And Jesus himself surely did not try to disabuse his disciples of thinking of him in kingly ways; just the opposite, he announced "the kingdom of heaven" as attached to his coming (Matt. 4:17) and proclaimed himself as ruler of a future kingly realm: "Jesus said to them, 'Truly, I say to you, in the new world, when the Son of Man will sit on his glorious throne, you who have followed me will also sit on twelve thrones, judging the twelve tribes of Israel'" (Matt. 19:28). And, in response to the question at his trial, "Are you the Christ, the Son of God?," Jesus replied, "You have said so. But I tell you, from now on you will see the Son of Man seated at the right hand of Power and coming on the clouds of heaven" (Matt. 26:63–64). Finally, the "King of kings and Lord of lords" who comes on the white horse, with eyes like a flame of fire and a sword coming from his mouth, conquers and reigns as king over all that stands against God (Rev. 19:11–21). Clearly, the Savior who comes as king comes only and necessarily as a man.

9) The incarnate mission and ministry of Jesus required that he come as a man. Yes, Jesus was the great and final prophet (cf. Heb. 1:1), priest (Hebrews 7–10), and king (Luke 1:32–33; Col. 1:13), and

for all these reasons he must have come as a man. But furthermore the very ministry Jesus conducted, calling out twelve male disciples, traveling with them over years of itinerate ministry, presenting himself broadly as a teacher of Israel, and challenging the religious leaders of the day, required that he be a man. It simply is inconceivable that, given the type of ministry the Father led his Son to perform, this could have been accomplished were the incarnate Savior, instead, a woman. While this point is true, it could be used wrongly, in my judgment. Upon considering that the ministry and mission of Jesus could not have been conducted in Israel as it was had the incarnate one been a woman, some might wish to conclude that this, ultimately, is *the reason* Jesus came as a man. After all, the social conditions were such that a woman as rabbi of Israel, rebuking the Pharisees, leading the disciples, etc., would have been fully unacceptable. Therefore, some might say, for these social and pragmatic reasons *only*, Jesus had to be a man.

Allow me three brief replies. (1) We have already considered eight reasons that the Savior who would come must be male, and three reasons yet follow. Clearly this is not the only (nor by any means the most important) reason our Savior had to be a man. (2) Is it reasonable to think that God would shrink back from challenging the socially unacceptable if he judged this would be best to do? Are we to think that the social conditions of Israel dictated to God the design and plan of the very incarnation itself? And (3) while it is true that those in Israel would expect, for example, the teacher of Israel to be a man, just why did they think this way? Was not the patriarchal system of Israel commanded by God himself? Was not the lineage of leadership in Israel established by God as being through sons in the line of David? Therefore, it seems entirely false to conclude that God's hand was somehow forced or even twisted by a culture's patriarchal mind-set of which he fundamentally disapproved. Rather, God designed male leadership and sent his Son as a man, functioning and ministering within the very overall patriarchal structure God himself established. Therefore, for social and cultural reasons, many of which were themselves established by God, our Savior had to be a man.

10) The Savior to come must have been a man because the risen Christ is now presented to the church not only as her Lord and king but also as her bridegroom. And, of course, in so doing, this echoes Yahweh's relationship to Israel. As the prophecy of Hosea illustrates beautifully, God intends his people to understand their relationship to him as that of a wife to her husband. Idolatry is depicted as adultery. And so God, as husband, requires fidelity and loyalty to him alone.

Similarly, the church is portrayed as the bride of Christ. The Revelation of Jesus Christ to John ends with several depictions of the church as the "bride" or "wife" of the Lamb (Rev. 18:23; 19:7; 21:2, 9; 22:17), and it is thereby clear that we are to understand Christ as the protector and purifier, while the church gives herself fully to him in obedience and love. All this depicts what marriage itself has meant from the beginning, according to Paul in Ephesians 5 (cf. 2 Cor. 11:2). When a wife submits to her husband as the church submits to Christ, and when a husband loves his wife as Christ loves the church, both reflect the two sides of the relationship of the church and Christ. Oh, what harm the false teaching of mutual submission in marriage produces. The parallel between a husband and his wife with Christ and the church simply will not allow the symmetrical kind of authority advocated by the voices favoring mutual submission. As Lord, king, head, and husband, Christ is fully and solely in charge over the church. As he made clear to us, we show our love for him when we do his commandments (John 14:15; 15:21, 23). There simply can be no mutual submission in terms of lines of authority between Christ and the church, lest we dishonor Christ's headship and rightful lordship over us. So too, the marriage relationship sees the husband in the role of Christ and the wife in the role of the church; authority is exercised by the former, submission by the latter. From this analogy, then, it is clear, that the Savior who would come to be the bridegroom of the church must have been a man.

11) It is necessary that our Savior be a man if he is to come as the Son of God. As we noted in our first point above, Jesus's role as Son indicates both his eternal relationship as preincarnate and eter-

nal Son of the eternal Father and as the incarnate one whose very life is brought about miraculously as he is born of a virgin. In answer to Mary's question, how she could bear this son, being a virgin, the angel tells Mary, "The Holy Spirit will come upon you, and the power of the Most High will overshadow you; and for that reason the child to be born will be called holy—the Son of God" (Luke 1:35). So, the eternal Son of the Father takes on human flesh by the power of the Most High and the eternal Son is born as the Son of God. It simply is inconceivable that this Savior could be born a woman. His sonship in eternity is matched by sonship in the incarnation, meaning that Jesus, our Savior, had to be born as a son (i.e., male).

12) Last, it is necessary that our Savior be a man if he is to come as the Son of Man. Jesus's preferred self-designation, clearly, was "Son of Man." This term occurs eighty-four times in the Gospels, every one of which is from the lips of Jesus himself, and nowhere do we find another naming him "Son of Man." His identity was wrapped up, in many ways, with the meaning of this term. And, without question, Jesus understood the background of this term in Daniel 7:13–14, for he refers to this Old Testament text as true of himself, in Matthew 24:30; 25:31; and 26:64. The Son of Man is presented before the Ancient of Days and is given "dominion and glory and a kingdom, that all peoples, nations, and languages should serve him" (Dan. 7:14); and this is none other than Jesus himself. And Jesus, knowing this incredible truth, amazes us even further when he uses "Son of Man" in other situations, as when he said, "For even the Son of Man came not to be served but to serve, and to give his life as a ransom for many" (Mark 10:45). Here, the royal and glorious Son of Man comes in humility and servitude, but he does so also knowing the day will come when his dominion will be exercised over all the earth (Matt. 26:64). So, both as the Son of Man who serves and suffers and as the Son of Man who rules and reigns, Jesus, the Son of Man, must have come to be our Savior as a man.

APPLICATION

So, here they are, twelve reasons why our Savior could not have been a woman and must have been a man:

1) Jesus Christ's preincarnate existence and identity is clearly revealed to be that of the *eternal Son* of the Father.

2) Jesus came as the second Adam, the man who stands as head over his new and redeemed race.

3) The Abrahamic covenant requires that the Savior to come, as the promised descendant of Abraham, would be a man.

4) The Davidic covenant (2 Samuel 7) explicitly requires that the one who will reign forever on the throne of David be a Son of David, and hence a man.

5) The new covenant of Jeremiah 31:31–34 requires that the Savior to come will actually accomplish the forgiveness of sins, and to do this, the Savior must be a man.

6) The Savior to come must be a prophet like unto Moses, as predicted by Moses and fulfilled in Jesus Christ, and so he must be a man.

7) Our new and permanent High Priest, whose office is secured as sins are atoned for and full pardon is pleaded on our behalf before the Father, must be a man.

8) Christ came also as the glorious King of kings, reigning over the nations in splendor and righteousness, and to be this king, he had to be a man.

9) The incarnate mission and ministry of Jesus required that he come as a man.

10) Because the risen Christ is now presented to the church not only as her Lord and king but also as her bridegroom, the Savior had to be a man.

11) Because our Savior came as the "Son of God" it was necessary that he come as a man.

12) Because our Savior came as the "Son of Man" it was necessary that he come as a man.

What implications and applications follow from this evidence of the necessity of our Savior's being not a woman but a man? Consider these three points in closing.

1) It is good for men and women that our Savior came not as a woman but as a man. Redeemed women, as well as men, must

acknowledge that their Savior was deliberately and intentionally, by God's wise plan and design, a man, not a woman. Given today's love affair with egalitarianism of many kinds, it may be more appealing for some to consider their Savior in generic human terms and remove from their consciousness, or at least from categories of theological significance, the fact that Jesus Christ of Nazareth was male. Perhaps his being male had as much significance as the fact that, in all likelihood, he also had dark eyes. In other words, while this may be true, of what importance is the observation? Now it should be clear that Jesus's being male was in fact theologically, Christologically, and soteriologically significant, despite what others have asserted. For reasons ranging from the nature of the Trinity itself to his role as the second Adam, the seed of Abraham, the son of David, the Son of Man, and the Son of God, Jesus simply had to be a man. And since his being male was by theological necessity, we should assent to its being good for all of us, men and women alike.

If some Christian women (or men) find this difficult to accept, I recommend two considerations. (1) Consider that this is God's eternal plan, devised in infinite wisdom for the well-being of those whom Christ has come to redeem. Knowing God's character as we do, or at least as we should, can we be at peace in our hearts and accept as good what God says is good? (2) Consider that redeemed men are hereby placed in a somewhat awkward position by this same truth, in that they must understand their identity as comprising part of the bride of Christ. How difficult it is for men to think of themselves as a bride. But, again, as we come to understand what this means, we see how good it is that Christ, the bridegroom, has called us—men and women, alike—to be his bride, to care and provide for, to purify and perfect, this object of his tender and everlasting love. In short, it is good for men and women that our Savior came not as a woman but as a man.

2) Jesus's male identity underscores the male headship that God built into human relationships. How can we miss something so obvious as this: Jesus's roles as king over Israel; Lord of the church; bridegroom and husband for his bride, the church—these all indicate the

role of male headship. To put the point differently, how can we maintain an egalitarian view of male-female relationships in light of the theological necessity of Christ's coming not as a woman but as a man? On the one hand, to *deny* the theological necessity of Christ's male identity would be unimaginably destructive to biblical theology and undermining of the very atoning work by which we are saved. On the other hand, to *affirm* the theological necessity of Christ's male identity entails an undergirding of male headship. So how can egalitarians reconcile the truth of Christ's male identity with their own egalitarian commitments?

3) Women need not fear that since Christ did not come as a woman, he cannot understand them, because in coming as a man, he came as a human being and so understands the human nature common to men and women alike. Much—perhaps too much at times—is made today of differences between men and women, and I don't deny that much of this discussion is valid. However, we must never forget the common human identity we all share, and with that the common kinds of fears, hopes, longings, aspirations, anxieties, weaknesses, and limitations that we share. Christ the man shared our (common) human nature so that men and women alike can have full confidence that he understands our plight (e.g., Heb. 2:18; 4:15–16). So, while Scripture clearly indicates Christ came as a man, and while our translations must continue to render accurately the masculine references to Christ everywhere they are found, we also realize that his coming as a man was therefore also as a human. As a man, he partook of our nature to live a human life and bear our sins. Christ the man, yes, but Christ in the human nature of every man and woman, also.

DISCUSSION QUESTIONS

1) Some might think that if Jesus had to be a man and couldn't have been a woman, then God favors men over women, and he considers men of greater value than women. Why is this conclusion wrong? What biblical teachings demonstrate God's equal love and care for women as for men?

2) Consider Galatians 3:26 along with Galatians 4:6–7. Both men and women who believe in Christ are referred to here as "sons" of God. Why should female believers not only not be offended by being called "sons" of God, but, even more, why should female believers, along with male believers, exult in being called "sons" of God? What clues from these verses help answer this question?

3) We know from Ephesians 5:31–32 that God designed marriage from the very beginning (Gen. 2:24) to be a picture of Christ and his bride, the church. Given this, how is it fitting that we should celebrate the "maleness" of Christ? And how can male believers, along with female believers, also celebrate our common role as the "bride" of Christ? What does this mean for all believers when we understand we are Christ's bride?

4) Consider the biblical idea of male headship, viz., that God has designed men to embrace positions of leadership in certain designated arenas, specifically in the home (Eph. 5:22–33) and the church (1 Cor. 11:4–10; 1 Tim. 2:12). In light of God's design of Christ's leadership as a man, in what ways should and does male headship exhibit Christlike leadership? And what happens to the picture of Christ's leadership over his bride, the church, when male headship is rejected and replaced with an egalitarian structure?

5) Consider 1 Corinthians 11:3. If there is authority and submission in the eternal relationship of the Father and the Son (the Father sends the Son, the Father creates through the Son, the Son always does the will of his Father, etc.), what implications does this have for authority and submission relationships that occur in the human sphere? Does it stand to reason that if there is authority and submission in the Godhead, God would create a world in which that same kind of authority and submission would be reflected? What biblical teaching do you see that bears this out?

7

DYING IN OUR PLACE

He himself bore our sins in his body on the tree, that we might die to sin and live to righteousness. By his wounds you have been healed.

1 PETER 2:24

The atoning death of Christ was only efficacious because Jesus who died for our sin was a full and integral human being. Now granted, he had to be more than merely a man to die for our sins. To be sure, he had to be the God-man for the atonement to be efficacious. But while he had to be more than a mere man, he could not have been less than fully a man.

THE ONLY TRUE SAVIOR IS TRUE GOD AND TRUE MAN

Although our focus is on Christ's humanity in the atonement, it is important to establish why Jesus had to be fully God for the atonement to "work," as it were. I recall a question that my daughter, Rachel, asked one evening as we were talking about the atonement. She inquired something along these lines: "Could God not have made a perfect second Adam who would bear our sin and die in our place? After all, if God had done this, we would have a perfect and sinless substitute sacrifice, one who like us was human, yet he wouldn't have had to send his own Son. So, why couldn't a perfect second Adam have been our Savior?" What a great question, and one that gets to the heart of why our Savior had to be the God-man. In short, the answer is this: if God had created a perfect and sinless second Adam, and if

God had worked in him so that he never sinned, this perfect man still could not have saved us by taking our sin and dying in our place. Why? As a man, he would qualify to take our place in death. But as only a man, he could take our sin and pay for it in just the same manner we, as "mere" humans, would pay for it.

So now the question is this: how do we, as humans, pay for our sin if we are required to pay for it ourselves? We pay for it eternally. That is, we never finish paying for our sin, because our sin requires an infinite payment. The reason that hell is eternal is simply that justice demands a full payment for our sin, and a full payment is impossible for finite humans to render to an infinitely holy God. Therefore, if we pay for our own sin, we pay forever, and hence there never comes a time when we can say, "It is finished!" It can never be said of us, "The payment for our sin has been completed, and God's just demands against us are fully satisfied!"

Now, let's return to our hypothetical second Adam. Since he is a man, but only a man, he would of necessity pay for our sin the same way the rest of us humans pay for our sin. So, were God to impute our sin to this sinless second Adam, and were he to die in our place for our sin, since he is merely human there never would be a time when he could declare, "It is finished!" Rather, this hypothetical second Adam would continue paying for our sin for all eternity, and hence, the guilt of our sin would never be forgiven, and the power of our sin would never be broken. Therefore, this hypothetical second Adam simply could not and cannot save us from our sin. We need a human substitute, to be sure. But we need a human whose payment for sin is of infinite value. Therefore, the only one who can save us from our sin is the sinless God-man—one who is fully man, as we are, but one who is fully God, so that his payment for our sin can satisfy the infinite demands of God's justice against our sin.

Therefore, Jesus had to be fully God as well as fully man. He had to be fully God for the payment he rendered to be of infinite value, satisfying fully the demands of an infinitely holy God against our sin. But he also had to be fully human in order for his death to be substitutionary, strictly speaking. He died in our place, dying the death we deserve to die, bearing in his body on the cross the sin we commit (1 Pet. 2:24), and to do this, Christ had to be a man. So although the infinite value of Christ's payment for our sin attaches to his being fully God, the substitutionary nature of Christ's death—that he took our place, bore our sin, and died the death we deserved to die—attaches most squarely to his being fully human. Once again, then, the atoning death of Christ was only efficacious because Jesus who died for our sin was a full and integral human being.

THE CENTRALITY OF PENAL SUBSTITUTION

Our evangelical faith, particularly as clarified and articulated in the Reformed tradition, holds the doctrine of penal substitution at the center of what we believe about the atonement.[1] "Substitution" refers to Christ's taking our place, i.e., substituting himself for us, in his death on the cross. "Penal" refers to the penalty he paid as he died in our place, taking our sin upon himself (2 Cor. 5:21) and paying the debt that we deserve to pay (Col. 2:14). And both of these elements are at the center of the atonement, as taught in Scripture, and both require that Christ who "died for our sin" (1 Cor. 15:3) was fully and truly human.

As for the centrality of penal substitution in the Bible's teaching on the nature of Christ's offering for us, consider Isaiah 53:4–6. Here is one of the richest and most glorious statements in all of Scripture on the nature of Christ's offering, and it clearly presents this offering as a substitute in our place and as a payment for our sin. Isaiah writes:

> Surely he has borne our griefs
> and carried our sorrows;
> yet we esteemed him stricken,
> smitten by God, and afflicted.
> But he was wounded for our transgressions;
> he was crushed for our iniquities;

---

[1] While penal substitution is understood as central to biblical teaching on the atonement in the Reformed tradition, this understanding of the atonement is disputed by many evangelical and non-evangelical scholars. For an overview of some of the range of opinion on this issue, see James Beilby and Paul R. Eddy, eds., *The Nature of the Atonement: Four Views* (Downers Grove, IL: InterVarsity, 2006).

upon him was the chastisement that brought us peace,
and with his stripes we are healed.
All we like sheep have gone astray;
we have turned—every one—to his own way;
and the LORD has laid on him
the iniquity of us all.

Both elements of penal substitution are given full expression in these verses. Notice that the servant here bears "our" griefs and "our" sorrows. He was wounded for "our" transgressions and crushed for "our" iniquities. Yes, his life and death were offered in place of ours. He took our place in what he accomplished on the cross, and in this he literally and truly was our substitute. But the reason for his being our substitute is found in the penal nature of his death. Notice that he was wounded for our "transgressions," crushed for our "iniquities." And in a manner that Paul will restate later in 2 Corinthians 5:21 ("For our sake he made him to be sin who knew no sin"), Isaiah here declares that "the LORD has laid on him the iniquity of us all" (Isa. 53:6). Yes, the Father laid our sin upon his Son, and hence the death that he died in our place (substitutionary) was a death in which he paid the penalty we deserved to pay (penal).

Some contemporary evangelicals have attempted to put penal substitution in a secondary position or to exclude it altogether in favor of some other biblical aspect of Christ's atoning work. Among those aspects put forward as more prominent, both historically and by some contemporary evangelicals, is the biblical teaching that Christ has conquered Satan and the forces of darkness through his death and resurrection. This *Christus Victor* theme of Scripture was upheld as the central motif of the atonement by some early church fathers and was brought back into the spotlight primarily through the work of Gustaf Aulén and followed by some more recent evangelical proponents.[2] While there is no question that the *Christus Victor* motif is a clear and glorious teaching of Scripture, and while Reformed evangelicals along with others celebrate the triumph of Christ over sin, Satan, demons,

---

[2] Gustaf Aulén, *Christus Victor* (London: SPCK, 1970). For a contemporary defense, see Greg Boyd's chapter in Beilby and Eddy, *Nature of the Atonement*.

and death, it nonetheless is a mistake to displace the centrality of penal substitution in the Bible's teaching on Christ's atoning work.

Perhaps a brief look at some of the key texts that support *Christus Victor* will help us see that while Christ's triumph over sin and Satan is gloriously true, it is only because his sacrifice was by nature a penal substitutionary offering that the accomplishment of the cross brought about this victory over the powers of darkness. Consider with me some key texts, then, where *Christus Victor* is taught but where penal substitution must also be understood as both true and central to account for the victory that Christ has won.

Arguably, the three most explicit texts in the New Testament expressing the truth that Christ has conquered Satan and all the powers of darkness are Colossians 2:15; Hebrews 2:14–15; and 1 John 3:8. These texts teach, respectively, that Christ has "disarmed the rulers and authorities and put them to open shame, by triumphing over them"; that Christ took on our human flesh that "through death he might destroy the one who has the power of death, that is, the devil"; and that "the reason the Son of God appeared was to destroy the works of the devil." These passages, along with a host of others—including importantly the Gospels themselves that portray Christ in conflict with the Devil, from his temptation in the wilderness to the Satan-inspired conspiracy of Judas and the Pharisees to put Jesus to death—all underscore the important theme that Christ, by his death and resurrection, conquered the very one who had the power of death, bringing this victory over Satan to Christ's followers and, in a broader sense, to the whole of the cosmos.

The question before us, then, is not whether the Bible teaches the *Christus Victor* theme, i.e., that Christ has conquered Satan and the powers of darkness. Indeed Scripture teaches this clearly, and its truth, spanning from Genesis 3:15 all the way through Revelation 20:10, is a major part of the broader biblical teaching of the efficacy of Christ's atoning death and victorious resurrection. Rather, the question before us is this: Is *Christus Victor* the central and most significant element among the aspects of the atonement, or should the penal substitutionary aspect of the atonement itself be seen as central, accounting for and giving rise to *Christus Victor*? In considering this question, I suggest that each of the three passages mentioned above, in its own context, indicates that penal substitution stands as the basis for *Christus Victor* such that the victory of Christ over Satan comes through, not apart from, Christ's paying the penalty for the sin of others by which (alone) Satan's hold on them is destroyed. In short, it seems clear from these texts that penal substitution grounds and accounts for *Christus Victor*, and that apart from penal substitution, *Christus Victor* simply would not and could not have happened.

The context of Colossians 2:15, where Christ is said to have disarmed the rulers and authorities, is one in which Christ's payment for the penalty of sin is first established before moving next to Christ's victory over Satan. In Colossians 2:13–14 we are told that in Christ we have been forgiven all our trespasses in that, by the very death of Christ on the cross, he canceled the record of debt that stood against us and set it aside, nailing it to the cross. The thrust in verses 13–14 is on expiation: the liability we owe before a holy God to suffer the penalty for trespassing his law has been removed ("forgiven" in v. 13; "canceling" and "set aside" in v. 14) as Christ took upon himself our record of debt and nailed it to the cross. The substitutionary death that Christ died, in which he cancelled out the debt of sinners, is the backdrop for the next glorious truth found in verse 15, where he disarmed the rulers and authorities, putting them to shame and triumphing over them. The death by which Satan is disarmed and put to shame, then, is a death that cancels our sin. These are not accidentally linked concepts but theologically and necessarily linked. The only way in which Satan could be defeated is as sin, which gave him the basis for his hold over sinners, was itself paid for, forgiven, and set aside. Christ's forgiveness through penal substitution is the means by which Christ conquered Satan's power.

Hebrews 2 likewise links Christ's destruction of Satan, who had the power of death (v. 14), with Christ's faithful priestly role in which he offered a propitiatory sacrifice for the sins of the people (v. 17). The common truth that links both effects is the incarnation: Christ shared in "flesh and blood" (v. 14), or variously, he was "made like his brothers" (v. 17) in order to accomplish these dual effects, to "destroy the one who has the power of death" (v. 14) and to "become a merciful and faithful high priest in the service of God, to make propitiation for the sins of the people" (v. 17). At the very least, it is clear that the *Christus Victor* theme does not stand alone; rather, it is deliberately linked to the theme of penal and propitiatory sacrifice. And when one asks, next, whether one has priority over the other, it would seem that the whole of the book of Hebrews suggests the answer. Clearly, the once-for-all sacrifice of Christ inaugurating the new covenant is presented in Hebrews as providing the payment for sin that was foreshadowed but never actually accomplished through the animal sacrifices of the old covenant (10:4). The stress in Hebrews on the sacrifice of Christ for the sins of the people clearly is the dominant note sounded in the book, and so it stands to reason that it (i.e., penal substitution) grounds the other important, yet dependent, truth that in this death for sin, he conquered the one who had the power of sin. Indeed, victory over Satan occurs only because the basis for his power (sin) is itself removed through penal and propitiatory sacrifice.

Finally, 1 John 3:4–10 shows that the Son of God's appearing "to destroy the works of the devil" (v. 8b) happens only as the very sins that are his "works" (v. 8) are themselves taken away through the sacrifice of Christ (v. 5). Similarly to Hebrews 2, we have here in 1 John 3:5 and 8 a dual purpose given for why Christ appeared: he appeared "to take away sins" (v. 5) and he appeared "to destroy the works of the devil" (v. 8). Both are true, but does one have priority over the other? Is one basic, so that as it occurs the second reality follows? Indeed the argument of 1 John 3:4–10 would suggest that only as Christ appears "to take away sin" does he, in so doing, take away the very sinful works that mark the Devil "from the beginning" (v. 8a) and by which Christ destroyed "the works of the devil" (v. 8b). *Christus Victor* occurs only as the very works that Satan carries out are themselves destroyed. What works are these? They are works of sin (v. 8a). So, as Christ comes to take away sin (v. 5), he destroys the sins that are the works of the Devil (v. 8b). Penal substitution, then, forms the basis by which *Christus Victor* is accomplished and secured.

Perhaps an analogy may assist in clarifying the point of Scripture's teaching here. Under a just system of laws of the state and judicial practice, a prisoner is locked in jail and his freedom curtailed precisely because he has been convicted of some crime whose penalty involves his incarceration. Notice that his *guilt* forms the basis for his *bondage*. Only because he has been proven guilty of breaking the law does the state have the right to put him behind bars. Furthermore, if a prisoner can prove his actual innocence, such that the charge of guilt can be removed—e.g., if some forensic or DNA evidence was forthcoming after his incarceration demonstrating his innocence—then the state would be obligated to free him from his bonds and release him from prison. Is it not clear, therefore, that the *power* of the state to withhold from people their freedom and put them in bondage comes from the *guilt* those very people have incurred and the accompanying just punishment directed at them as a result? Remove the *guilt* and you remove the just basis for *bondage*.

Similarly, Satan's power over sinners is tied specifically and exclusively to their guilt through sin. His hold on them is owing to their rebellion against God in sin and his subsequent jurisdiction over their lives as a result of that sin. But remove the guilt through Christ's payment for their sin and you remove the basis for Satan's hold on them! So it is through Christ's death that, as he took upon himself the sin of others and paid the full penalty for their sin, the rightful hold that Satan had upon them is necessarily broken and the basis for this bondage is removed. Remove the guilt and you remove the bondage; accomplish penal substitution and you accomplish *Christus Victor*. Therefore, as glorious as the truth of *Christus Victor* is, the truth that makes possible and necessary Christ's conquering of Satan and his power is the more central and foundational truth that Christ paid the penalty for our sins through his penal and propitiatory sacrifice. Penal substitution grounds *Christus Victor*. Praise be to our Savior for this gracious forgiveness of our sin and guilt that accomplishes also this glorious deliverance from Satan's dominion and bondage (Col. 1:13–14).

PENAL SUBSTITUTION AND THE HUMANITY OF CHRIST

With the centrality of penal substitution to the atoning work of Christ in mind, we now consider some of the ways in which Christ's humanity was necessary for his atoning death actually to remove our sin. And here it may help our reflection to use the categories of "substitute" and "penalty"—the component parts of the doctrine of penal substitution—to think through the importance of Jesus's humanity for the atonement.

First, for Jesus to be our substitute, he had to be truly and fully a man. Hebrews 2:14 makes this very point: "Since therefore the children share in flesh and blood, he himself likewise partook of the same things, that through death he might destroy the one who has the power of death, that is, the devil." Nothing less than one who shared fully in our "flesh and blood," i.e., our human nature, could in fact atone for sin and bring victory over Satan. A couple factors should be considered to see this more clearly.

1) The substitute sacrifices that had been offered under the old covenant clearly were not human sacrifices. Rather, God required animal sacrifices, with certain specifications about what kind of animals and their quality and the like. But one might wonder, if God was able to use animal sacrifices in the old covenant to substitute for the sins of his people, why not continue that practice and avoid having to sacrifice a human being? The answer is simple, and it is found in Hebrews 10:4: "For it is impossible for the blood of bulls and goats to take away sins." What may be surprising to many of us is this realization: none of those Old Testament animal sacrifices actually paid for any sins of believing Israelites, and hence, none of those Old Testament sacrifices were in themselves efficacious. How, then, could God forgive those Old Testament saints on the basis of the animal sacrifices they brought, indeed, those sacrifices that they were commanded by God to bring, if in fact it was impossible for any of them actually to take away sin?

The answer is astonishing, and it brings us to Jesus, the one-and-only sacrifice that actually could atone for our sin. The efficacy of those Old Testament animal sacrifices rested not in themselves but altogether in what they pointed to. They were "types" of the greater sacrifice that was to come. They pointed to the planned and purposed and certain coming of "the Lamb of God" (John 1:29), whom the Father would offer for the people, the divine-human Lamb who would actually remove the sin of all those who believed the promises of God. In other words, those animal sacrifices required in the old covenant, while they had no ability in themselves actually to pay for any sin whatsoever, were efficacious precisely because they were connected in the divine mind and plan to the future once-for-all sacrifice that would be rendered when Jesus came and died on the cross.

A helpful analogy is to consider what happens when you buy something with a credit card. Suppose you're in the mall, and you find some shoes you like. You can take those shoes up to the register, charge them to your credit card, and walk out of that store with your new shoes, having paid absolutely nothing for them! Why is this not shoplifting? Why are you not stopped at the door by the security guard and charged with stealing? You are free to leave with the shoes because you have entered into a legal transaction whereby you have obligated yourself to a future payment by which you (and others) may now consider those shoes as your own. Even though you have not yet paid a penny for them, you have tied yourself legally to an agreement (that's what you've done, by the way, when you sign the credit card slip) by which those shoes will be paid for by you at some agreed-upon date in the future. So, while the shoes are legally yours, they are only paid for when the credit card statement comes and a payment is made from your bank account.

In a similar way, God forgave the sin of all Old Testament saints, as it were, on credit. He devised a system of sacrifices by which each of those animal sacrifices would signal his obligation, at some point in the future, to ensure that the payment for those sins would surely and truly be made. In other words, in order to forgive those Old Testament saints at that point in history, he had to put in place a plan by which their sin, pronounced forgiven by him then, would one future day actually and fully be paid for. Apart from that future payment, those animal sacrifices were totally useless.

This is the reality that stands behind the declaration and demonstration of God's righteousness that Paul extols in Romans 3. Recall the words of Paul, that God brought forth his Son as a payment for sin "to show God's righteousness, because in his divine forbearance he had passed over former sins. It was to show his righteousness at the present time, so that he might be just and the justifier of the one who has faith in Jesus" (Rom. 3:25b–26). Do you see the point? God "passed over former sins" every time he forgave a believing Israelite, in the old covenant, who brought an animal sacrifice to atone for his sin. So when will God actually demonstrate that he was righteous in forgiving those sins? How is it not the height of legal treachery for God to declare those Old Testament saints forgiven (e.g., Gen. 15:6) when none of their sins had actually been paid? The answer comes in Romans 3:26. At the coming of Christ and his death on the cross, God demonstrated that he is righteous to forgive sin, since the payment for all sin, for all time, was made in and through the work of his Son. The credit card statement has come, the check is written, and the payment has been accepted! This is what God has done in the offering of his Son, who alone could make the payment in full for our sin.

All this is to say that the sacrifice for our sins could not be the animal sacrifices that were offered repeatedly throughout the old covenant. It was and would remain "impossible for the blood of bulls and goats to take away sins" (Heb. 10:4). So God provided one who came sharing our "flesh and blood" (Heb. 2:14) as a man, and this sacrifice alone could truly and actually substitute for us in paying the penalty for our sin.

2) Another reason our substitute had to be of our "flesh and blood" is that he had to come as the second Adam and succeed where the first Adam failed. In both Romans 5 and 1 Corinthians 15 Paul develops the parallels between Adam and Christ. One of the key elements in this comparison is the observation that through "one man" (Rom. 5:12) sin and death entered into the world, so through "one man Jesus Christ" (v. 15) salvation and righteousness would be regained. As we

will develop more in the next chapter, Christ came as the second Adam in part to win back what was lost by Adam. Adam's sin had brought upon him and all of his posterity not only the guilt of sin, which had to be paid for by this second Adam, but also the bondage of sin and Satan by which we lived under their dominion. Christ came to "break the power of cancelled sin" by delivering us from the tyranny of Satan.

This glorious truth is declared in the words of Colossians 1:13, where Paul writes of all those who now are forgiven in Christ, "He has delivered us from the domain of darkness and transferred us to the kingdom of his beloved Son." Or, as Hebrews 2:14 likewise states, "Since therefore the children share in flesh and blood, he himself likewise partook of the same things, that through death he might destroy the one who has the power of death, that is, the devil." The second Adam, Christ, paid for our sin and by this eliminated the hold that Satan had upon us. We are forgiven and set free; sin's penalty has been paid and sin's power is now broken. Through this "one man Jesus Christ," we are delivered and liberated from sin and death, never to be subject to Satan's deadly bondage again. Only because Jesus was a man, the second Adam who obeyed his Father and lived his righteous life, would his death for us secure both the full payment of our sin's guilt and the full deliverance from sin's awful tyranny.

Additionally, only this "flesh and blood" substitute could actually pay for sin in a way that none of the animal sacrifices of the old covenant ever could do (Heb. 10:4). Only Jesus as a man could truly be the substitute we need. But there is more to consider, particularly when one contemplates the penalty Jesus bore on the cross as he died for our sin. Two aspects of his death for our sin relate directly and significantly to his humanity, in particular.

1) As Peter states, when Jesus died on the cross he "bore our sins in his body on the tree" (1 Pet. 2:24). Or as Paul indicates, "For our sake he [the Father] made him [the Son] to be sin who knew no sin, so that in him we might become the righteousness of God" (2 Cor. 5:21). So, as Jesus hung on that cross, he "bore our sins" to such an extent that the Father "made him to be sin." As we saw earlier from Isaiah 53:4–6, it was "our transgressions" and "our iniquity" that he bore on

the cross. He who was in himself sinless took on our sin as he died on the cross.

Theologians sometimes use the word *imputation* to refer to the charging of our sin to Christ. In fact, there are three "acts" of imputation in the history of redemption. Adam's sin was imputed (charged) to all of Adam's posterity when he sinned (Rom. 5:12ff); our sin was imputed to Christ on the cross (2 Cor. 5:21); and Christ's righteousness, by faith, is imputed (credited) to those who believe (Rom. 4:4–5; 2 Cor. 5:21). Here we're concerned with the second act of imputation. The Father actually charges his own Son with our sin and guilt in order that he might pay for them and secure for us the forgiveness and righteous standing that we then receive by faith. This is the heart of the gospel, and it is the heart of the work of Christ on the cross.

Christ had to be human in order for this imputation of our sin to take place. If he were divine only, it is inconceivable and impossible that our sin would be imputed to him. How could his eternal sinless and holy nature take on sin? As God, he is unchangeable in his perfection (Heb. 1:10–12; 13:8) and infinite in his holiness (e.g., the thrice-holy God of Isaiah 6:1–4 is rightly a vision of Christ, as indicated by John 12:41). No, the divine nature cannot be tarnished with sin, and certainly as God (only), Jesus could not have been "made sin." But the Father *did* make him to be sin, and he *did* bear our sin in his body on the cross. Clearly, then, the imputation of our sin to Christ has in mind his full and perfect humanity that was, at the moment of this imputation, made what it never had been before—sin. Allow these words to penetrate: at a moment on the cross, when the Father imputed our sin to his Son, in his human nature the previously sinless Jesus was made sin. Only because he was fully and truly human (as well as fully and truly divine) could this imputation of our sin to Christ have occurred.

2) Paul writes, "The wages of sin is death" (Rom. 6:23). What naturally follows the imputation of our sin to Christ, then, is clear. Because the Father imputed our sin to his Son, and because the penalty of that sin is death, what occurred next simply had to occur: "Christ died for our sins" (1 Cor. 15:3). His death was real because the

sin imputed to him was real, and the penalty for that sin was divinely mandated. Yes, the sinless Son of God come in human flesh bore our sin in his body on the cross, and died as a result.

The relation of Christ's death for our sin to his humanity should be clear. Because he bore our sin in his humanity, it was the humanity of Jesus, in particular, that was subject to death. After all, God cannot die. God is eternal, and self-existent and possesses life in himself. So, it is impossible, strictly speaking, for God, as God, to die. But if God (the Son) takes on human nature, then it becomes possible for God, as man, to die. This is the sense in which we must sing the refrain of Charles Wesley's glorious hymn "And Can It Be?" As the volume increases and voices join to extol, ". . . that thou, my God, shouldst die for me," we must have in mind that this is true, but only because in this case God (the Son) has been joined with human nature so that God dies only as the human nature joined to the divine nature dies on that cross. God, as God, cannot die. But God the Son, as man, died indeed.

Perhaps it would be helpful to think a bit about ways in which we talk about Christ in relation to some of the activities of his life. Some activities are tied, strictly speaking, only to one or the other of his two natures, and it is important that we discern this in order not to misunderstand either Christ's deity or his humanity. For example, when Jesus said, "I thirst" (John 19:28), clearly this was an expression of his human nature. The divine nature, as self-sufficient and spiritual, has never been thirsty and cannot be thirsty. But a human nature, as we all know, can indeed become thirsty. So we can rightly say: (a) the human nature in Jesus became thirsty, or (b) Jesus, the God-man, became thirsty. But we would err were we to say (c) the divine nature in Jesus became thirsty. Or consider Jesus's forgiving of sin (e.g., Mark 2:1–12), an action that only God can do (as the scribes rightly concluded; Mark 2:7). So, of this action of forgiving sin, we can rightly say: (a) the divine nature in Jesus was capable of and brought about forgiveness of the paralytic's sin, or (b) Jesus, the God-man, was capable of and brought about forgiveness of the paralytic's sin. But we would err were we to say (c) the human nature of Jesus was capable of and brought about forgiveness of the paralytic's sin.

In like manner, when we contemplate the imputation of sin to Jesus and his subsequent death, we must be careful how we think about these aspects of his work on the cross as they relate to his two natures. We can rightly say (a) the human nature of Jesus bore our sin and died on the cross, or (b) Jesus, the God-man, bore our sin and died on the cross. But we would err were we to say (c) the divine nature of Jesus bore our sin and died on the cross. In neither case is the divine nature susceptible to either sin or death. In order for Jesus to bear our sin and die for us, he had to be fully and truly a man.

APPLICATION

1) Realize that the ultimate reason that Jesus became a man was to do exactly the two things we have just focused upon—bear our sin and die on the cross for us. Yes, of course, much else was done by Jesus, and many other reasons round out the fullness of why he came to earth. But at the heart of his coming, at the core of his choosing to follow the will and plan of his Father and take on our human nature, was this purpose: to bear our sin and die. As Jesus articulates his own mission, "For even the Son of Man came not to be served but to serve, and to give his life as a ransom for many" (Mark 10:45).

What an amazing truth—the eternal Son of the Father left the glories of heaven and took on our human nature for one ultimate, pervasive, and central purpose: to bear the sin we have committed and to die the death that we deserve, because he knew that only in this way would we be saved. Marvel at this love. Marvel at this sacrifice. And worship this God become man.

2) Learn to discipline your thinking about Jesus when it comes to his being both fully God and fully man. To paraphrase James, the path of wisdom here is to be "quick to hear" but "slow to speak." That is, we should be quick and eager to hear the Word of God repeatedly while being slow and measured in what we conclude about Jesus's

two natures. The mysteries of the hypostatic union—i.e., the union of two *ousia* (natures) in one *hypostasis* (person)—match those of the Trinity, and we dare not jump to quick and easy judgments. Arius, the foe at Nicaea and proponent on the Son as the creation of the Father, erred exactly at this point. When he read that Christ did not know the hour of the second coming (Mark 13:32), he concluded that he could not have been God. He reasoned, God certainly knows all things, but here Jesus declares that he doesn't know some particular thing, therefore Jesus cannot be God. The problem, of course, is precisely with Arius's misunderstanding of the two natures of Christ. Because Jesus lived his life as a man and limited the expression of many of the divine attributes required for such integral human life, there were many things that he had to learn as he grew, and some things were never revealed to him. So the limitation in knowledge that Jesus experienced was real, but it was a function of his human nature. As God, he knew (and knows) everything there is to know. So we would be right to say (a) the human nature in Jesus was ignorant of the time of the second coming, or (b) Jesus, the God-man, was ignorant of the time of the second coming. But we would err were we to say (c) the divine nature in Jesus was ignorant of the time of the second coming. It was precisely the failure of Arius to contemplate these complexities that led him to his heretical conclusions. God grant us grace to be quick to hear (his Word) and slow to speak (our judgments).

3) Consider again the categories of "substitute" and "penal" as they relate to our condition before God. Realize that Christ, and Christ alone, is the only substitute who can adequately represent us in his offering on our behalf. And realize that Christ alone made the payment that fully and eternally satisfied God's wrath against our sin. That Christ is the one who fulfilled what we need most through his penal substitutionary sacrifice merits our everlasting adoration, praise, worship, and allegiance. With Paul we affirm that we have indeed been bought with an unspeakably great price, and therefore it is only right that we should glorify God in our bodies (1 Cor. 6:20).

DISCUSSION QUESTIONS

1) Consider the importance of the doctrine of the penal substitutionary atoning death of Christ. What do the words *penal* and *substitution* contribute to our understanding of this doctrine? What passages of Scripture express aspects of this central truth about the atoning death of Christ for our sin?

2) Other aspects of the atonement taught in Scripture include Christ's death, which is a "sacrifice" offered for our sin, a death which "redeems" or "purchases" us from the penalty of our sin, and a payment that "propitiates" the Father's wrath against us due to our sin. Consider how Christ's death as penal substitution is related necessarily to his death as a sacrifice, as a redemption, and as a propitiation for our sin.

3) Reflect on the importance of the humanity of Christ in relation to his bearing our sin and dying for us. Only as a man could he have our sin imputed to him; and only as a man could he die for our sin. How does this truth enlarge your praise and honor of Christ, who took on our human nature precisely to bear our sin and die for us? In what ways does his taking on of human nature actually increase the love we already have for the eternal Son of the Father?

4) When Jesus suffered on the cross, he bore all of our sin in his agonizing death for us. Consider for a moment, to the extent you can, the fullness of the sin you have committed in your life—every action, attitude, word, and thought that brought displeasure to God and violated his standards of righteousness. Think of the horror of that sin, how ugly and dark and distressing that sin is. Now realize that Jesus bore *all* of your sin in his body on the cross. Further, he bore the "sin of the world" (John 1:29) when he died on the cross. Ponder the magnitude of the love the Father and the Son have for us sinners as you contemplate the horror of the sin Christ bore and the penalty he paid.

5) What are some ways our lives should reflect that we have been bought with a price (1 Cor. 6:20)? Of what significance is it that Jesus died for our sin? And what difference should this make in how we act toward others? How should his death for sinners affect our witness in the world? Just what does it mean that we have been redeemed by the blood of Christ?

8

RAISED, REIGNING, AND RETURNING IN VICTORY

. . . that he worked in Christ when he raised him from the dead and seated him at his right hand in the heavenly places, far above all rule and authority and power and dominion, and above every name that is named, not only in this age but also in the one to come. And he put all things under his feet and gave him as head over all things to the church, which is his body, the fullness of him who fills all in all.

EPHESIANS 1:20-23

The Scriptures are filled with the glorious teaching that Jesus Christ, who died for our sin, was raised from the dead and is now seated at the right hand of the Father, exercising his reign over all things. When the fullness of the Father's purposes are accomplished on earth and the Son has built his church fully according to design, this risen and exalted Lord Jesus Christ will come again, defeating all the enemies of God and ushering in the fullness of his kingdom on a restored earth. In short, Jesus who died has been raised from the dead, is reigning over all, and will return as King of kings and Lord of lords, to live with his bride forever.

These three inseparable realities—the resurrection, reign, and return of Christ—provide great hope and confidence to the followers of Christ, and all three are tied directly to the humanity he bore as he became incarnate. After all, it is the humanity of Jesus that was raised from the dead, and it is in the humanity of Jesus that he is exalted to the Father's right hand to reign over all, and it will be in his humanity that he returns to earth just as the disciples watched him go (Acts 1:11).

Of these three claims—that the humanity of Jesus is tied inextricably to his resurrection, reign, and return—perhaps it is the middle truth that some might wonder whether it should be attached, in the same kind of a way, to the humanity of Christ. Surely his *resurrection* is clearly related to his human nature, for he died in his humanity and was raised bodily from the dead. And surely the *return* of Christ is related to his humanity, for he will come bodily and physically (albeit in a glorified body, of the sort that we, too, will be given in the resurrection at his coming) to triumph over God's enemies and take his bride to himself forever. But isn't the *reign* of Christ now—the power and authority he exercises, and his dominion over Satan and all the powers of creation—a function principally of his deity? Doesn't he reign now as God the Son more directly than as a man per se?

We will examine this interwoven triad of truths regarding Christ, the raised, reigning, and returning King. Of the three, we devote special attention to the second, given that here we may have more questions regarding the relevance of his humanity to his current function as the exalted and reigning Lord. What we will see is that all three areas are deeply and inextricably tied to the humanity of Christ such that our hope for what is to come in the consummation of all things is dependent upon the fact that this Jesus is none other than the second Adam, the seed of Abraham, the greater son of David, who as a man was raised and exalted to carry out the work the Father designed for him to do. Consider with me, then, the relevance of the humanity of Christ for this triad of glorious truths, that Jesus Christ who died has been raised from the dead, is reigning now over all, and will return to establish peace and justice forevermore.

RAISED FROM THE DEAD

We begin with one of the most important and glorious of all biblical truths, that the Christ who died for our sin has succeeded in paying sin's penalty and conquering sin's power as evidenced by his being raised from the dead, never to die again. It is important here to see the connection between the efficacy of the death of Christ for our sin and the truth of his subsequent resurrection. After all, Paul begins his gospel explanation in 1 Corinthians 15 by declaring that "Christ died for our sins" (v. 3), only to say just a bit later that "if Christ has not been raised, your faith is futile and you are still in your sins" (v. 17). One wonders, then, if Christ's death is what deals with our sin, why does it matter whether he rises from the dead or not? After all, it is in his death that our sin is dealt with, right? So, why does Paul insist that if Christ has not been raised, we are still in our sin? Another way to put the question is this: how is the efficacy of Christ's death for sin tied to the necessity of his resurrection? Or, for Christ's death for our sin truly to have worked, why is it necessary that Christ subsequently rise from the dead? This does seem to be what Paul is indicating, but why?

To see the answer, consider with me two features of sin. Sin is for all of us a twofold problem. Sin presents us with a penalty that we cannot pay and a power that we cannot overcome. And, interestingly, if we inquire just what that penalty is, and what sin's strongest power is, we find that we come to the same answer. As Paul says in Romans 6:23, the wages of sin is death. So it is clear that the penalty that sin brings to each one of us is death. And if one considers for a moment the power that sin has over us, we realize that its power is manifold. It can urge us to greed, anger, pride, lust, murder, and many more horrific states of mind, attitude, and action. But in all of these we have some capacity to fight back, as it were. We can resist, to some degree, those urges of sin in all of those ways. But the one power that sin has over us to which we have no recourse is death. This is its final and greatest power about which we can do nothing whatsoever. So it is clear: sin's penalty is death, and sin's greatest power is death.

Now back to 1 Corinthians 15:3, "Christ died for our sin." If Christ died for our sin, and sin is to us both a penalty we cannot pay and a power we cannot overcome, then Christ's death for our sin must both pay sin's penalty and conquer sin's power. But since sin's penalty is death, if it is true that Christ has "died for our sin," what is the necessary expression that Christ has paid the penalty of sin fully? He *must* rise from the dead. If he remains in a grave dead, then the penalty of sin is still being paid, and thus its payment has not been made fully.

And what about sin's power? If Christ has "died for our sin," and sin's greatest power is death, then what is the necessary expression that Christ has conquered the power of sin completely and decisively? He *must* rise from the dead. If he remains in a grave dead, then sin's power is greater than his, and rather than conquering sin, he is subject to it and its hold on him. The only way to show that the power of sin is conquered completely is that Christ was raised from the dead. This shows that Christ's power is greater than the greatest power sin has. Christ's resurrection demonstrates that Christ has completely, decisively, and once for all triumphed over sin and its greatest power!

Does it matter, then, that Christ has truly and literally been raised from the dead? Yes, as Paul himself intimated, the resurrection is the only way in which the efficacy of Christ's atoning death for sin can be demonstrated. His death for sin worked, we might say, as his resurrection proves.

Given the importance of this doctrine to the whole of our Christian faith, we must realize again how critical it is that Jesus was fully human. Just as God *as God* cannot die, so God *as God* cannot be raised from the dead. But in Jesus, the God-man, we see that God *as man* has died for our sin, and likewise God *as man* has been raised from the dead. The atoning death of Christ requires his full humanity, and the resurrection of Christ does likewise.

One other important connection of the humanity of Christ to his resurrection bears mentioning. The Bible's doctrine of the resurrection pertains not only to the resurrection of Christ. As important as Christ's resurrection is, there is more to the story—the biblical storyline of our salvation. Another glorious part of the story is this: Christ is the firstfruits of those raised from the dead, so that all who have believed in him will likewise be raised (1 Cor. 15:20–23). Although we know little about the resurrected and glorified body of Jesus, we know that his glorified human existence has become the pattern for our future life. As Christ was raised, so shall we be, and so our hope both for life after death, and for human life at its pinnacle, is rooted in the resurrection of Jesus himself. His humanity is the pattern for our own, and as he reigns forever in his glorified human state, so we will reign as glorified humans alongside him. The hope we have of a future fullness of human existence is connected necessarily and inextricably to the fullness of the humanity of Jesus, whose humanity is the pattern and prototype for our own.

REIGNING OVER ALL

The risen Jesus, who appeared to many of his disciples in a variety of different settings, soon became the ascended and exalted Lord. Jesus's ascension into heaven, to sit at his Father's right hand, is one of the most important yet neglected areas of Christology. Just what is involved in the current reign of the risen Christ, and does this aspect of his life and work relate directly to his humanity?

If one looks carefully at biblical teaching about the current reign of Christ over all things, it seems clear that one must conclude that he is reigning as a man who has won the right to rule over the world he has purchased and conquered. Our intuition that led us to think of the present reign of Christ as the reign of the divine Son is called into question as we reflect on many passages that speak of his current position and activity. What we find instead is that the one who reigns has authority over the nations that he lacked previously, and rights over all powers in heaven and earth that he won through his obedient life and death on the cross, and a position of supremacy granted him by the Father that he has only now in his ascended state.

In other words, these biblical teachings do not fit well the notion that the reign of Christ is conducted principally and fundamentally out of his divine nature. How could you say of the divine Son per se that he is *given* authority over the world, or that he is *granted* the nations as his possession? After all, did not the divine Son create this world, and does he not have intrinsic authority over it as God and creator? Yet we find in Scripture over and over again language that indicates the "newness" of the position Jesus now has and of the authority that Jesus now exercises. Such "newness" has no appropriate "fit" with the deity of Christ, but it surely does with this human Son, this Messiah, this son of David, who is granted as his reward the rulership of the world he has won and conquered. Consider with me some key passages that lead to this conclusion.

First, consider the royal or inaugural psalm of David, Psalm 2. The key section, for our purposes, asserts:

> Then he will speak to them in his wrath,
>   and terrify them in his fury, saying,
> "As for me, I have set my King
>   on Zion, my holy hill."
> I will tell of the decree:
> The LORD said to me, "You are my Son;
>   today I have begotten you.
> Ask of me, and I will make the nations your heritage,
>   and the ends of the earth your possession.
> You shall break them with a rod of iron
>   and dash them in pieces like a potter's vessel." (vv. 5–9)

The context for this portion of the psalm is the description of the nations of the world that are rebelling against God and his anointed Son (vv. 1–3). They chafe at his laws and despise his rulership. God, for his part, laughs at them (v. 4), but then his laughter turns to anger. In his fury, the Lord—who must be understood as the Father, since he speaks to and about his Son—installs his King on Zion and announces his long-standing decree of who this king is and what he shall do. The king is none other than his own Son, whom he begets at this point in history as his Son. And then he instructs his Son, "Ask of me, and I will make the nations your heritage, and the ends of the earth your possession. You shall break them with a rod of iron and dash them in pieces like a potter's vessel" (vv. 8–9). The Lord as Father of this Son offers to give the nations to the Son, to grant him the ends of the earth as his possession. The Son, for his part, is not given these nations to save them but to bring cataclysmic judgment upon them. As we see this text fulfilled in Revelation 19 at the return of Christ, this triumphant king and Lord will indeed smite the nations and bring them to death and ruin. The nations are his, then, because the Father grants them to him, and they are his to conquer through divine warfare. A few observations are important.

First, the reference in Psalm 2 to the "begetting" of this Son cannot refer either to the eternal begetting of the eternal Son or to the time of the incarnation, when the Son was begotten in the womb of Mary. There are two reasons for seeing this as yet a third point at which the Son "becomes" Son in a new sense—viz., in his resurrection and ascension. (1) The first is the simple observation that what this begotten Son does, according to Psalm 2:9, is to bring to them condemnation and destruction. But this was not true of the Son as the eternal Son who created the nations, nor was this true of the incarnate Son who came to save the nations. Recall the sober words of John 3:17, that "God did not send his Son into the world to condemn the world, but in order that the world might be saved through him." But this Son of Psalm 2 is given the nations precisely and specifically to do the opposite of what he did in his first coming. He will come to those nations in judgment, executing the fury and anger of his Father. So this "sonship" is not of his eternal sonship, nor of his incarnate sonship, but rather the sonship granted him as the risen, ascended, exalted, and reigning King of kings and Lord of lords. (2) The second reason for seeing the Son of Psalm 2 as the risen and exalted Son is that this is precisely how Paul understood this text. In Paul's sermon recorded in Acts 13, he refers to the resurrection of Jesus as the basis for the fulfillment of what was promised and foretold in Psalm 2. Paul says, "And we bring you the good news that what God promised to the fathers, this he has fulfilled to us their children by raising Jesus, as also it is written in the second Psalm, "You are my Son, today I have begotten you" (Acts 13:32–33). This begotten Son, then, is neither the eternal Son nor the incarnate Son born of Mary but the risen Son who is raised and exalted to reign over the nations.

Second, though obvious, we need also to point out that according to this psalm, the Father *makes* the nations his heritage and the ends of the earth his possession. This indicates two important truths. (1) The Father has ultimate authority over his Son and carries out his will in and through his Son. Just as the heavens and earth were created by the Father through his Son, and just as the salvation of the nations occurred as the Father sent his Son to die for the sin of the world, so too here, the Father executes his final and climactic judgment on the rebellious nations of the world through the actions of his Son. After all, it is the wrath and anger of the Father that is expressed here, even though the instrument that displays that wrath is the Son, King Jesus. (2) As this Son is begotten in his resurrection and exaltation, he now is given these nations as his inheritance, indicating that he did not have them before. But could this be said of the eternal Son who created those nations? Could this be said of the divine (only) Son of the Father? No, this statement only makes sense of the Son when seen as one who is given what he lacked, whose reward for his work is to receive this inheritance. This refers to the human Son who came through the line of Abraham, David, and Mary. This human Son did not have intrinsic rights to those nations but is given rights over them, to carry out the Father's will for them, because he is the begotten Son of the resurrection and ascension.

Third, there is no question but of the victory of the Son over these nations. Although they rage against God, their raging will prove vain (even as Ps. 2:1 has intimated). The anger of the Father will be satisfied as the Son executes relentless judgment on the nations, dashing them "in pieces like a potter's vessel" (v. 9). And when we look at the prophesied fulfillment of this psalm, recorded for us in Revelation 19, we are confirmed in our conclusion that the Son will abide no foe or allow any to live who rage against God in the end. As King of kings and Lord of lords, he will accomplish his divinely ordained and decreed purpose, and his will be a thorough and exacting victory.

Fourth, marvel that the psalm calls those very judges and nations raging against God to recognize the folly of their ways and bow before the Son before it is too late (Ps. 2:10–12). What mercy God shows toward these very ones who are the objects of his wrath and indignation. This leads us to well up with gratitude for a first coming of this Son, which prepares for his second coming. In his first coming, the wideness of God's mercy is manifest as his Son dies for the world and offers salvation to any and all who believe. But in his second coming, the fury of God's judgment is manifest as his Son—the one and very same Son who died for the nations—now takes up his sword and smites the nations in their ongoing idolatry and rebellion against their creator God. Although God announces the certainty of this coming judgment, he does so in part to persuade rebels to drop their arms and bow to Jesus as their personal Lord and king. What mercy that precedes such horrific destruction. How infinitely kind of God to plan this first coming of Christ rather than to move directly to the substance of the second.

Now, all of these observations are reflections on the reigning and ruling of the triumphant Son, who is fully and truly human. It is the human Jesus who is given the nations as his inheritance, the human Jesus who takes up the sword of judgment, and the human Jesus who comes again to break those nations with a rod of iron. Marvel, if you will, that all of this is true of one who is fully and truly human. Although sent by the Father, and although possessing the divine nature, he nonetheless carries out his work in the power of the Spirit and does so as the man, the second Adam, whom God made him to be.

For our second passage, consider afresh the Great Commission our Lord gave to his disciples:

> And Jesus came and said to them, "All authority in heaven and on earth has been given to me. Go therefore and make disciples of all nations, baptizing them in the name of the Father and of the Son and of the Holy Spirit, teaching them to observe all that I have commanded you. And behold, I am with you always, to the end of the age." (Matt. 28:18–20)

Often Matthew 28:19–20 is quoted without any particular attention given to the preceding statement from Jesus. In verse 18 Jesus says something quite astonishing. Rather than declaring what me might otherwise expect—something along the line of "All authority in heaven and earth is and always has been mine alone," or "All authority for all eternity has been mine since I created the heavens and the earth"—he says this: "All authority in heaven and on earth *has been given to me*" (Matt. 28:18). Amazing! Simply astonishing! Right away we realize, as we give this a few moments' reflection, that Jesus cannot be speaking here about the inherent authority he would have over all of creation by virtue of being the creator of all that is. Clearly, as creator, all things are under his authority and are subject to his rule. As God, Jesus cannot be given authority over heaven and earth, for he possesses this authority by divine right. So this must be the authority given to him in his humanity. He is granted what he did not have before, and so now, having been given this authority, he sends his disciples to the nations over which he now has absolute authority and rights of rulership.

A related incident helps us see this. Recall that one of the three recorded temptations Satan brought to Jesus was to take him to a high place where he could see all the kingdoms of the world. Luke 4:5–7 records for us, "The devil took him up and showed him all the kingdoms of the world in a moment of time, and said to him, 'To you I will give all this authority and their glory, for it has been delivered to me, and I give it to whom I will. If you, then, will worship me, it will all be yours.'" Isn't it interesting that Satan said to Jesus that he (Satan) possessed the nations as his own, that they had been "delivered" to him? Furthermore, isn't it also fascinating that Satan now offered these nations, along with authority over them, to Jesus? Of all people, he offers these nations to Jesus, who, as God, created those nations!

Now, if it were not true that Satan had these nations as his own possession, and if instead it were true that Jesus possessed these nations, certainly Jesus would have challenged him on this offer. He would have exposed the legitimacy of what Satan was offering as a lie. But Jesus does not challenge the offer Satan makes. Rather, he challenges the *terms* of the offer. Recall that Satan had set as the condition for Jesus's receiving the nations and authority over them that he (Jesus) must worship Satan. So, hear now Jesus's reply to Satan: "And Jesus answered him, 'It is written, "You shall worship the Lord your God, and him only shall you serve"'" (Luke 4:8). In other words, Jesus would not accept the terms of the offer (worshiping Satan), although he never disputed the legitimacy of the offer itself. In fact, Satan was too smart to try to tempt Jesus with a bogus offer. He would not get anywhere with an offer that Jesus could see through as false.

The truth is that Satan offered to Jesus what he had, and the temptation was forceful because what Jesus was offered—the nations of the world—was exactly what Jesus had come to secure. But the pathway that the Father designed for Jesus's receiving the nations was the pathway of the cross. He must live a fully obedient life, take upon himself the sin of the world, and die a death of unspeakable torment and pain. All of this could be avoided simply by bowing before Satan and receiving the nations in a quick, easy, painless way. Yes, Satan possessed the nations, as God has granted him that authority due to Adam's sin. Yes, Jesus came to win the nations as his own through the pathway of obedience, suffering, and death. And so, yes, this was a real and forceful temptation.

When Jesus declares, then, in Matthew 28:18 that "all authority in heaven and on earth has been given" to him, he is speaking from the other side of the cross; he declares this as the risen and victorious Messiah. Through his obedient life and death for sinners, Jesus qualifies to receive the nations and full authority over them. Jesus in his humanity—as the seed of Abraham, the son of David—announces that the nations are his. And to his disciples he commands, as it were, "Go get them! They're mine." It is the human Jesus who is given a kind of authority he didn't have before, and it is the human Jesus who commands his disciples to go in his name. As the Messiah who bought the nations with his shed blood on the cross, he receives rightly full authority over those nations to bring into his fold all of those the Father has given to him. Marvel, then, that the Christ of the Great Commission is the human Jesus, the Messiah, who has won the right to reign over the nations.

A third passage we'll consider briefly is found in Paul's prayer at the end of Ephesians 1. Here, Paul writes that the Father has

> raised [Jesus] from the dead and seated him at his right hand in the heavenly places, far above all rule and authority and power and dominion, and above every name that is named, not only in this age

but also in the one to come. And he put all things under his feet and gave him as head over all things to the church, which is his body, the fullness of him who fills all in all. (Eph. 1:20–23)

We see again here what we've seen elsewhere. The Father is in the position of highest authority, and he grants to his raised and exalted Son the place of second in command—"at his right hand." And from this position, the Son exercises absolute authority over everything created—"above all rule and authority and power and dominion, and above every name that is named, not only in this age but also in the one to come." That the Father grants him this position and authority is made clear in verse 22, where we see that the Father is the one who "put all things under his feet and gave him as head over all things to the church." In other words, this is not a position of the eternal Son of the Father, who, as creator of all that is, has intrinsic authority and absolute divine rights. Rather, this authority is delegated to the messianic Son. From this position he now rules with uncontested and indefeasible might, but that he has this position is owing to the Father's will to exalt his God-man, this greater son of David, to this highest of all positions, over all and under only the Father himself.

Two additional passages connect conceptually to what Paul says here in Ephesians 1, and these simply reinforce the truths we've just seen. Notice in Philippians 2:9–11 that the exalted Son is the one who was obedient to the point of death, even death on the cross. So we read, "Therefore God has highly exalted him and bestowed on him the name that is above every name, so that at the name of Jesus every knee should bow, in heaven and on earth and under the earth, and every tongue confess that Jesus Christ is Lord, to the glory of God the Father" (Phil. 2:9–11). Notice three things: (1) The "therefore" that begins verse 9 connects what was described in the previous verses to the action now taking place. Because of the faithfulness of this incarnate Son, because of his humble obedience in going to the cross, God highly exalted him. His position of honor and authority was not his position as the eternal Son of the Father but as the obedient incarnate Son, the human Messiah. (2) The Father is the one who bestows on his

Son both his exalted position by which all created beings will bow the knee and confess Christ's lordship with their tongue, and the "name that is above every name," showing his supreme position over all of creation. (3) That the Father exalts the Son, and the Father gives to his Son his superior name, indicates the ultimate place of authority and supremacy held by the Father alone. This is reflected even in how the Son is praised by all of creation. For every knee will bow and every tongue will confess that Jesus Christ is Lord. But there is no period following this declaration. Rather, the confession that Jesus is Lord redounds to the glory of the Father, since he is in the highest of all positions from which he has made his Son the delegated ruler over all creation.

There is, then, such a fitting correspondence between the pictures given in Ephesians 1:20–23 and Philippians 2:6–11. The Son is the obedient, incarnate, raised, and exalted human Son, and his exaltation is to a position he has earned by his life and work. So although he is fully God as well as fully man, this exaltation has to do fundamentally with the accomplishment of his human life now rewarded as the Father grants him dominion over all he came to subdue.

The other corresponding text worth glancing at is 1 Corinthians 15:27–28. Paul writes, "For 'God has put all things in subjection under his feet.' But when it says, 'all things are put in subjection,' it is plain that he is excepted who put all things in subjection under him. When all things are subjected to him, then the Son himself will also be subjected to him who put all things in subjection under him, that God may be all in all." We see here again the same basic themes we've observed in Ephesians 1 and Philippians 2. By the Son's victorious death and resurrection, he is given a position he did not have before. Following the resurrection and ascension of the Son, God (the Father) puts all things in creation in subjection under the feet of this triumphant Son. But because the Father does the subjecting, he is not himself one of those made subject to the Son. No, the Father is subject to no one and nothing. But the Son, now under only the Father, is given the position of supreme authority over all, even as he willingly and gladly subjects himself to the Father, "that God [the Father] might be all in all."

Although we won't take time to discuss other texts, it might be helpful to notice that these truths about the exaltation of the obedient, incarnate Son, following his humble death for sin and triumphant resurrection, are expressed in many other passages. Notice the following, paying special attention to the italicized portions as well as to the specific persons indicated (see brackets for clarification):

> A Psalm of David.
> The LORD [the Father] says to my Lord [the Son]:
> *"Sit at my right hand,*
> *until I make your enemies your footstool."*
> *The Lord sends forth from Zion*
> *your mighty scepter.*
> *Rule in the midst of your enemies!*
> Your people will offer themselves freely
> on the day of your power,
> in holy garments;
> from the womb of the morning,
> the dew of your youth will be yours.
> *The LORD has sworn*
> *and will not change his mind,*
> *"You are a priest forever*
> after the order of Melchizedek." (Ps. 110:1–4)

> I saw in the night visions,
> and behold, with the clouds of heaven
> there came one like a son of man [fulfilled in Christ],
> and he came to the Ancient of Days [the Father]
> and was presented before him.
> *And to him was given dominion*
> *and glory and a kingdom,*
> *that all peoples, nations, and languages*
> *should serve him;*
> his dominion is an everlasting dominion,
> which shall not pass away,
> and his kingdom one
> that shall not be destroyed. (Dan. 7:13–14)

> For to this end Christ died and lived again, *that he might be Lord* both of the dead and of the living. (Rom. 14:9)

Long ago, at many times and in many ways, God spoke to our fathers by the prophets, but in these last days he has spoken to us by his Son, *whom* [the Son] *he* [the Father] *appointed the heir of all things*, through whom also he created the world. He is the radiance of the glory of God and the exact imprint of his nature, and he upholds the universe by the word of his power. After making purification for sins, *he sat down at the right hand* of the Majesty on high. (Heb. 1:1–3)

But we see him who for a little while was made lower than the angels, namely Jesus, *crowned with glory and honor because of the suffering of death*, so that by the grace of God he might taste death for everyone. (Heb. 2:9)

[Jesus Christ] has gone into heaven and is *at the right hand of God, with angels, authorities, and powers having been subjected to him.* (1 Pet. 3:22)

Suffice it to say, then, that Scripture uniformly teaches that the exalted Son, who sits at the right hand of the Father, to whom all authority in heaven and earth has been given, and who reigns over all, building his church and awaiting the day of his return in judgment— this Son is none other than the incarnate Son who was born of Mary. Receiving this position and authority, which he did not possess previously, over all of creation applies not to the eternal Son per se but to the incarnate, human, Son of God. We see, then, a human Jesus who is raised from the dead, and the same human Jesus who has ascended and received from the Father absolute authority over all of creation. His delegated but absolute authority over "all rule and authority and power and dominion" (Eph. 1:21) testifies to the Father's ultimate place over all and to the derived authority of this Son, due to his faithfulness, obedience, and victorious death for sin.

RETURNING IN VICTORY

As the human Jesus was raised from the dead and exalted to the place of highest authority over all creation, so this same human Jesus will return bodily to earth. Evangelicals have long defended both the bodily resurrection of Christ and his bodily return. As the angel told the disciples when they saw him ascend into heaven, "Men of Galilee, why do you stand looking into heaven? This Jesus, who was taken up from you into heaven, will come in the same way as you saw him go into heaven" (Acts 1:11). Yes, we rightly await and long for the day when Jesus will come again, and this Jesus who comes will be the same incarnate Son, born of Mary, returning in his glorified body to receive all who are his.

The return of Christ is the source of greatest hope for believers, but it should likewise be the source of deepest dread for unbelievers. There never will be a time in history marked by such contrasts. How could believers be more joyful than at the moment they see Jesus descend to take them to be with himself forever? But, oh, what destruction and horror will befall the whole of the world as this victorious Son comes to wield the wrath of his Father in the judgment of the nations. And, yes, it is the human Jesus in whose likeness we will be perfectly made at his coming (1 John 3:1–2), and it is the human Jesus who comes as warrior to judge and destroy all who stand against their creator (Rev. 19:11–21).

How amazing to contemplate Jesus in his humanity at his return. Yes, he is fully the God-man, fully God and fully man from the moment of his conception in Mary and forevermore, without end. But just as it was his humanity in particular that was the focus of his resurrection, and in his human nature he was exalted by the Father to a position he did not have previously, so here in his return his humanity has primacy. He comes as the God-man, to be sure, but he comes particularly as the victorious son of David, king and Lord, who now is finishing the work the Father decreed from eternity past that he do. He brings his followers into their new home with him, and made like him, forever, and he destroys the rebellious with the sword that comes from his very mouth. As saving Lord and victorious king, this is the glorified human Jesus in his return. And what glory he will display!

APPLICATION

Although there are many applications of these glorious truths, we'll limit our reflection here to one key area of application for each of the triad of truths we've examined.

1) The single most glorious reality about the resurrection of Christ is what it demonstrated! The horrific penalty of our sin forgiven fully and the crushing power of sin conquered completely—these are the realities demonstrated and proven when Christ walked out of that tomb alive from the dead! What strength this should give to us who are in Christ, knowing that there can be no outstanding accusation of guilt that can jeopardize our right standing with God, since our justification by faith is based solely on the perfect and complete work of Christ. Furthermore, the more we meditate on these truths and allow them to take root in our hearts and souls, we should have a growing confidence that since Christ has conquered all of sin, including sin's greatest power through his resurrection from the dead, there is no abiding sin in our life over which Christ cannot—indeed, does not—reign supreme. Indeed, he has broken the power of canceled sin, and this should grant to those in Christ a basis for strong prayer, earnest hope, and longing expectation, even as we struggle with powerful sin that remains in us day by day. The greater power, though, is Christ's. And may we always rely on him to do in us what only he can do, because he has been raised from the dead.

And of course, the fullness of the effects of Christ's resurrection for our lives as his followers is yet to be seen. We live now in the period of the "not yet," in which bodies decay and sin remains although fully forgiven and conquered. But the day is coming when faith will become sight and the glories of the fullness of his resurrection work will be realized. Oh what joy we rightly anticipate as he makes all things new! Our hope is not based on fickle and frail political alignments or financial holdings or relational dealings. What vain hope, were this the case. No, our hope is based on the surety and certainty of the resurrection that will come. When Christ descends from heaven with the shout of the archangel, we will be raised to the fullness of the human lives the Father always intended us to have in his Son. And then we will see the full flowering of the effects of Christ's death and resurrection over sin—everlasting forgiveness, everlasting wholeness of life, everlasting purpose and fulfillment—because of the everlasting righteous reign of the risen Christ. Oh Christian, we have every reason to hope, not despair. Because Christ is risen, and we one day with him, let us don this hope and joy.

2) Let us take this truth to heart: Christ was exalted to the right hand of the Father and given his place of authority over all creation *because* he was "obedient to the point of death, even death on the cross" (Phil. 2:6–11). What we see here is, no doubt, the most glorious illustration ever lived out of the principle articulated in James 4:10: "Humble yourselves before the Lord, and he will exalt you." Jesus lived the most obedient life ever lived, seeking always to do the will of his Father who sent him, suffering greater pain as the cost of his obedience than anyone ever has or could experience. But this was his reward: "Therefore God has highly exalted him" (Phil. 2:9). Clearly the measure of his humble obedience became the measure of his glorious exaltation. "God is not mocked, for whatever one sows, that will he also reap" (Gal. 6:7). In the most positive way possible, this was lived out beautifully in Jesus.

Let us learn from the divine principle lived fully and perfectly in Jesus's life that God will not fail to honor those who honor him, that he will exalt those who are humble, that he will reward obedience in ways beyond our comprehension. Oh, how our obedience matters! So, how wrong it is of us to appeal to grace as license to disobey, just as it is equally wrong to appeal to our obedience as the basis for our right standing before God. If we could just get Ephesians 2:8–10 (i.e., not just vv. 8–9) all together, we would be in such better shape as Christian people. Yes, we are saved by grace, through faith, fully and completely apart from works. But our salvation apart from works breeds a life filled with good works, which God prepared for us to do. May God grant us longing of heart to live more fully as Jesus lived. May we see that just as his relentless and perfect obedience, rendered in the power of the Spirit and in faith, brought him the full approval of his Father and the reward of his exaltation, so our obedience, rendered in the power of the Spirit and in faith, likewise will be seen and rewarded by our gracious and benevolent God. Let us learn from Jesus that obedience matters.

3) As we await the return of Christ, may we contemplate more deeply the truths of his righteous victory than the horrors of this world's sinful failures. We are surrounded with evil and hatred and cruelty and suffering, and it is easy to despair in the face of pervasive wickedness. But to do so is to fail to see and believe what is more deeply true and fundamental than all of the terrorist plottings and schemes throughout history. Christ has triumphed, and he is coming to bring peace and righteousness to earth. In this we have hope, and in this we rejoice. The crucified and risen Savior, now reigning at the right hand of the Father, surely and certainly is coming again, and when he does, all wrongs will be made right and all evil brought to an end. These truths should be the ointment for the sores that have wounded our souls. May we relish the greatest hope there is, that Jesus, the victorious son of David, son of Mary, is coming again. Come quickly, Lord Jesus!

DISCUSSION QUESTIONS

1) When you consider some of the most common temptations that we face in our culture—material acquisition, immediate gratification, popularity and pleasing others—what are some ways in which the triumph of Christ over sin, death, and Satan put these temptations into new perspective? How does the certainty of his eternal reign over all things transform how we think about the pull of these kinds of temptations?

2) How do you respond to the truths that the resurrection of Christ declare—the penalty of our sin has been paid fully and the power of our sin has been conquered completely? What difference does this make in your estimate of Christ? And what difference does this make in understanding your daily, ongoing fight against sin?

3) Recall Ephesians 1:18–23. When you consider the present reign of Christ over all rulers, authorities, and powers, how should this affect how you read your daily newspaper? What difference should this make in how we interpret world events? How should this affect our zeal for missions? Just what differences does it make that Christ indeed reigns?

4) When you wake up in the morning, are you consciously aware that Jesus is coming again? Do you recall that it could be today? If we brought this truth to mind regularly, what difference would this make to our priorities? To how we spend our money? To the activities we commit to? To the time we spend serving others? If we consciously remembered each day that Jesus is coming again, how might this transform our perspectives on life?

5) How grateful are you that the eternal Son of the Father came to earth, in obedience to his Father, to become a man? What central truths about the life, the ministry, and the mission of Christ are only explained by virtue of his being fully and authentically a man? What strength do you find in the realization that there is one mediator between God and man, the man Christ Jesus? Consider the humanity of Christ and revel in the multitude of reasons why it is crucial that our Savior be one who is both fully God and fully man.

GENERAL INDEX

"And Can It Be?" (Wesley), 124

Anselm, 91

applications to the Christian life: of Jesus
dying in our place, 125–26; of Jesus as
a male human being, 107–9; of Jesus as
the Spirit-anointed Messiah, 43–45; of
Jesus's growing human wisdom, 55–57;
of Jesus's kenosis (self-emptying),
27–28; of Jesus's obedience, 27–28,
69–71; of Jesus's resurrection, reign,
and return, 144–47; of Jesus's temptations, 87–88

Arius, 75, 126

atonement. *See* imputation (of our sin to
Jesus); Jesus, dying in our place; penal
substitution

Augustine, 75n6, 96, 96n6

Aulén, Gustaf, 114, 114n2

Bavinck, Herman, 74–75, 81, 75nn5–6, 78

Beilby, James, 113n1

Berkhof, Louis, 74, 74n3

Boyd, Greg, 114n2

"A Brief Summary of Concerns About the
TNIV" (Grudem), 93n5

Christology (O'Collins), 77n14

Christus Victor (Aulén), 114n2

church, the, as the bride of Christ, 105

Council of Constantinople III (680), 75

covenant: Abrahamic covenant, 99–100;
Davidic covenant, 100–101; the new
covenant, 101

creation, 24–25

Cur Deus Homo (Anselm), 91

DeWeese, Garret J., 81n19

divine (enabling) gifts, 89

Dogmatic Theology (Shedd), 75, 75n8

Eddy, Paul R., 113n1

Erickson, Millard, 25n2, 61, 61n1, 78–79,
78n15, 81

faith, fight for, 70–71

Flint, Thomas P., 78n16

"fruit of the Spirit," 35, 46

Great Commission, 42–43, 137–38

Grudem, Wayne, 93n5

Harris, Murray J., 13n1

Hawthorne, Gerald F., 34, 34n1, 79n17

Hebrews, book of, stress of on the sacrifice
of Christ, 117

humility, 56–57

hypostatic union (the union of two *ousia*
[natures] in one *hypostasis* [person]),
126

imitatio Christus, 45

imputation (of our sin to Jesus), 123–25;
three "acts" of in the history of redemption, 123

isa (Greek: equality), 18; Paul's use of in
Philippians 2:5–8, 18–19, 20

Issler, Klaus, 77n14

Jesus: as both fully divine and fully
human, 15–24, 28, 32–33, 111–13; as
the church's bridegroom, 105, 107,
108; conception of in the Virgin Mary,
15–16, 32, 50, 106; dying in our place
(*see also* penal substitution), 111–26,
127; as the eternal Son of the Father,
95–98, 107; as the final and permanent
High Priest in the order of Melchizedek,
102, 107; genealogies of, 100; growing
human wisdom of, 47–54; humility

of, 44, 56–57; impeccability of, 73n1, 79–85; the incarnate mission and ministry of, 103–4, 107; kenosis (self-emptying) of, 16–24, 28; as King of kings, 102–4, 107; as the "Lamb of God," 120; as a male human being, 91–106; as the "man of sorrows," 101, 107; miracles of, 37n2; obedience of, 24–26, 28, 59–71, 72, 88; as the promised descendant of Abraham, 32, 99–100, 107; as a prophet like unto Moses, 101–2, 107; as the Psalm 1 prototype, 53, 84; reign of, 129–30, 133–43; resources he used to live his obedient life (the Word of God, prayer, the community of faith, the Spirit), 43–44, 45, 84–85, 88; resurrection of, 129–30, 130–33; return of, 129–30, 143–44; as the second Adam, 32, 98–99, 107, 121–22; as "Son" (the eternal Son, the incarnate and historical Son, the risen and triumphant Son), 15n1; as the Son of David, 32, 100–101, 107; as the "Son of God," 105–6, 107; as the "Son of Man," 106, 107; as the Spirit-anointed Messiah, 33–43; temptations of, 73–86, 138–39. *See also* hypostatic union (the union of two *ousia* [natures] in one *hypostasis* [person]); imputation (of our sin to Jesus)
"Jesus' Example: Prototype of the Dependent, Spirit-Filled Life" (Issler), 77n14
Jesus as God: The New Testament Use of Theos *in Reference to Jesus* (Harris), 13n1
John the Baptist, conception of in Elizabeth, 50

kenoō (Greek: to empty or pour out), 19; Paul's use of in Philippians 2:5–8, 19–20

Lewis, C. S., 15
"living like Jesus," 27
The Logic of God Incarnate (Morris), 77n13
Lombard, Peter, 75n6

male headship, 98, 108–9, 110; and marriage, 105

marriage: God's design for, 110; and male headship, 105
McKinley, John E., 79n17
Messiah, the, Old Testament prophecies concerning, 40
Moore, Russell D., 79n17
morphē (Greek: inner nature or substance of something), 17; Paul's use of in Philippians 2:5–8, 17–18, 20, 23
Morris, Thomas, 77, 77n13, 78

The Nature of the Atonement: Four Views (ed. Beilby and Eddy), 113n1
New International Version (NIV), rendering of the gender of Jesus in, 93–95
The New Testament and Psalms: An Inclusive Version (ed. Gold et al.), on the gender of Jesus, 92, 92n1
nominalists, 75

obedience, 28, 69, 72; resources for living an obedient life (the Word of God, prayer, the community of faith, the Spirit), 43–44, 45, 88
O'Collins, Gerald, 77, 77n14
"One Person, Two Natures: Two Metaphysical Models of the Incarnation" (DeWeese), 81n19
Osterhaven, M. E., 73n2

Pelagius, 75
penal substitution: centrality of, 113–18; the *Christus Victor* theme, 114–18; and the humanity of Jesus, 119–25; and Jesus's death as a sacrifice, as a redemption, and as a propitiation for our sins, 127; meaning of "penal," 113; meaning of "substitution," 113
Plato, on "forms," 17
"The Possibilities of Incarnation: Some Radical Molinist Suggestions" (Flint), 78n16
The Presence and the Power: The Significance of the Holy Spirit in the Life and Ministry of Jesus (Hawthorne), 34, 34n1, 79n17

Reformed Dogmatics (Bavinck), 75n5
resurrection of the dead, 132–33, 145–46

Satan: conquering of through Jesus's death, 114–18; and Jesus's temptations, 85–86, 138–39; power of over sinners, 118

Shedd, William G. T., 75–77, 75n8, 78, 79, 80, 81

sin, 127, 131

"Sinlessness of Christ" (Osterhaven), 73n2

"sons" of God, 110

Spirit and Word connection, 55

submission, 56–57

suffering, 69–70, 71, 72

Systematic Theology (Berkhof), 74n3

temptations: common temptations in our culture, 147; resources for fighting temptations (the Word of God, the community of faith, prayer, the Spirit), 45, 87, 88

Tempted and Tried: Temptation and the Triumph of Christ (Moore), 79n17

Tempted for Us: Theological Models and the Practical Relevance of Christ's Impeccability and Temptation (McKinley), 79n17

theological discussions, 55–56

Today's New International Version (TNIV), rendering of the gender of Jesus in, 93–95

Trinity, the, 23; authority and submission inherent in, 96–97, 98, 110

The Trinity (Augustine), 96n6

Wesley, Charles, 124

Who's Tampering with the Trinity? An Assessment of the Subordination Debate (Erickson), 25n2, 61n1

The Word Became Flesh: A Contemporary Incarnational Christology (Erickson), 78n15

worked-out righteousness, 27–28, 146

SCRIPTURE INDEX

Genesis
2:24	110
3:6	98
3:9	98
3:15	115
12	99
12:2–3	99
15	99
15:3–5	99
15:4	99n7
15:6	121
17	99
17:16	99
17:19	99

Exodus
8:10	18
15:11	18

Deuteronomy
3:24	18
18:15	101

2 Samuel
7:12–13	100
7:22	18

1 Kings
8:23	18

Psalms
1	53, 84
2	134, 135
2:1	136
2:1–3	134
2:4	134
2:5–9	134
2:8–9	134
2:9	135, 136
2:10–12	136
22	53
45:6–7	103
71:19	18
110:1–4	142

Isaiah
6:1–4	123
9:6–7	40, 103
11	36, 40
11:1–3	34–35, 41, 51
11:1–4	41
11:2	35, 51
11:4	41–42
42:1–4	39, 41
42:2–3	41
46:9	18
46:10	70
53	36, 54
53:4–6	101, 113–14, 122–23
53:6	114
53:9	80
53:10	101
53:12	101
61	36
61:1–3	51

Jeremiah
31:31–34	101
31:34	101
49:13, 18	97

Ezekiel
34:23–24	100
35:9	97
36:27	39
37:24–28	100

Daniel
7:13–14	106, 142
7:14	106

Obadiah
10	97

Micah

7:18	18

Malachi

1:6	97

Matthew

1	100
4:17	103
11:1–6	40
11:25–27	92
12:24	36
12:28	36
14:22–23	37
16:16	37
17:1–13	33
19:28	103
20:28	24
24:30	106
25:31	106
26:36–46	65
26:38	66
26:63–64	103
26:64	106
28:9, 17	37
28:18	137–38, 139
28:18–20	137–38

Mark

2:1–12	32, 124
2:5ff	81
2:7	124
9:2–13	33
10:45	106, 125
13:32	126
14:32–42	65

Luke

1:15	50
1:26–35	15–16
1:31	16
1:31–33	101
1:31–35	15n1
1:32	16
1:32–33	103
1:35	16, 50, 106
2	50
2:40	49, 49–50, 54, 57, 80
2:40, 52	47, 49
2:41–51	47
2:46–47	47
2:48	47–48
2:49	48
2:50	48
2:51	56
2:52	49, 54, 57, 80
3	100
4:2	81
4:5–7	138
4:5–8	85
4:8	138
4:14	35
4:17–21	35–36
9:28–36	33
22:21	101
22:39–46	65
22:42	67
22:44	65

John

1:1	15n1, 18
1:14	96
1:29	120, 127
1:33–34, 49	15n1
3:16–17	15n1
3:17	25, 42, 96, 135
6:37–38	95
6:38	25, 62, 63n2
6:44	96
8:28–29	63
8:42	62, 63n2
11:1–16	33
11:25	33
12:41	123
14:15	105
15:10	59
15:21, 23	105
16:14	14
19:28	81, 124
20:26–29	37

Acts

1:1–2	42
1:2	42
1:8	39
1:11	129, 144
3:22	102
10	37
10:38	31, 37, 37n2, 38, 39, 84
13	135
13:32–33	15n1, 135

Romans

1:3–4	15n1
3	121
3:25b–26	121
3:26	121
4:4–5	123
5	121
5:12	98, 121
5:12ff	123
5:12–19	98
5:12–21	98
5:15	98, 121
5:16	98
5:17	98
5:18	98
5:19	98
6:23	123, 131
14:9	142

1 Corinthians

6:20	126, 127
8:6	24
11:3	110
11:4–10	110
11:7–9	98
11:25	101
15	121
15:3	68, 123, 131
15:17	131
15:20–23	132
15:21–22	94, 98, 98
15:27–28	15n1, 141

2 Corinthians

5:21	80, 113, 114, 122, 123
8:9	24
11:2	105

Galatians

2:20	15n1
3:14	100
3:16	100
3:26	110
4:4	15n1, 96
4:6–7	110
5:22–23	35, 46
6:7	146

Ephesians

1:11	70
1:18–23	147
1:20–23	129, 139–40, 141
1:21	143
1:22	140
2:8–9	146
2:8–10	145
5	105
5:18	58
5:19–20	58
5:22–23	97, 110
5:31–32	110

Philippians

2:5	27, 29, 32
2:5–8	15, 17
2:5–9	27
2:6	17, 18
2:6–11	141, 146
2:7	17, 18, 19
2:8	24, 25, 25n2, 62–63n2, 68
2:9	140, 146
2:9–11	140
2:11	14

Colossians

1:12–16	96
1:13	103, 122
1:13–14	118
2:13	116
2:13–14	116
2:14	113, 115, 116
2:15	116
3:16a	58
3:16b	58

1 Timothy

2:5	11, 12, 33, 94–95
2:12	110
2:13–15	98

Hebrews

1	102
1:1	103
1:1–2	15n1, 24, 96
1:1–3	143
1:3	18
1:10–12	123
2:9	143
2:14	116, 117, 119, 121, 122
2:14–15	115
2:17	91, 116, 116–17, 117

2:18	109	*2 Peter*	
4:14	15n1	1:20–21	46
4:15	63, 71, 73, 74, 78, 80,	2:24	111, 113
	88	3:18	37
4:15–16	109		
5:7	60, 61, 65	*1 John*	
5:7–9	59	3:1–2	144
5:8	60, 61, 71	3:4–10	117
5:8–9	60	3:5	80
5:9	67–68	3:8	115, 117
7	102	3:8a	117
7–10	103	3:8b	117
7:27–28	102	4:9–10	15n1
10:4	117, 119, 121, 122	*Revelation*	
13:8	123	18:23	105
		19	134, 136
James		19:7	97, 105
1:13	74	19:11ff	42
4:10	146	19:11–21	103, 144
		20:10	115
1 Peter		21:2, 9	97, 105
2:21	31	22:17	105
2:21ff	44		
2:21–22	80		
2:21–23	11–12		
2:24	122		
3:22	143		

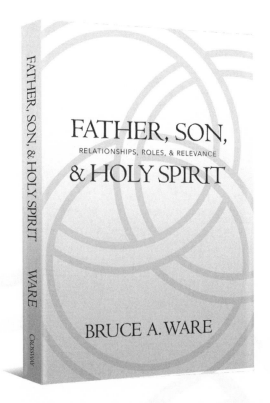

BEHOLDING THE
WONDER OF OUR
TRIUNE GOD

Bruce Ware provides an approachable examination of the doctrine of the Trinity. He discusses the relationship and roles of the Father, Son, and Holy Spirit and the practical implications of the Trinity for our lives. A great study for you and your home, church, and ministry.

Visit crossway.org for more information.